Debating the Future
of American Education

Brookings Dialogues on Public Policy

The presentations and discussions at Brookings conferences and seminars often deserve wide circulation as contributions to public understanding of issues of national importance. The Brookings Dialogues on Public Policy series is intended to make such papers and commentary available to a broad and general audience. The series supplements the Institution's research publications by reflecting the contrasting, often lively, and sometimes conflicting views of elected and appointed government officials, other leaders in public and private life, and scholars. In keeping with their origin and purpose, the Dialogues are not subjected to the same formal review procedures established for the Institution's research publications. Brookings publishes the contributions to the Dialogues in the belief that they are worthy of public consideration but does not assume responsibility for their objectivity and for the accuracy of every factual statement. And, as in all Brookings publications, the judgments, conclusions, and recommendations presented in the Dialogues should not be ascribed to the trustees, officers, or other staff members of the Brookings Institution.

Debating the Future
of American Education:
Do We Need National Standards
and Assessments?

Edited by

DIANE RAVITCH

Report of a conference sponsored by the Brown Center on

Education Policy at the Brookings Institution

THE BROOKINGS INSTITUTION / Washington, D.C.

ℬ THE BROOKINGS INSTITUTION

The Brookings Institution is an independent organization devoted to nonpartisan research, education, and publication in economics, government, foreign policy, and the social sciences generally. Its principal purposes are to aid in the development of sound public policies and to promote public understanding of issues of national importance.

The Institution was founded on December 8, 1927, to merge the activities of the Institute for Government Research, founded in 1916, the Institute of Economics, founded in 1922, and the Robert Brookings Graduate School of Economics and Government, founded in 1924.

The Board of Trustees is responsible for the general administration of the Institution, while the immediate direction of the policies, program, and staff is vested in the President, assisted by an advisory committee of the officers and staff. The by-laws of the Institution state: "It is the function of the Trustees to make possible the conduct of scientific research, and publication, under the most favorable conditions, and to safeguard the independence of the research staff in the pursuit of their studies and in the publication of the results of such studies. It is not a part of their function to determine, control, or influence the conduct of particular investigations or the conclusions reached."

The President bears final responsibility for the decision to publish a manuscript as a Brookings book. In reaching his judgment on the competence, accuracy, and objectivity of each study, the President is advised by the director of the appropriate research program and weighs the views of a panel of expert outside readers who report to him in confidence on the quality of the work. Publication of the work signifies that it is deemed a competent treatment worthy of public consideration but does not imply endorsement of conclusions or recommendations.

The Institution maintains its position of neutrality on issues of public policy in order to safeguard the intellectual freedom of the staff. Hence interpretations or conclusions in Brookings publications should be understood to be solely those of the authors and should not be attributed to the Institution, to its trustees, officers, or other staff members, or to the organizations that support its research.

Preface

On May 18, 1994, a group of scholars, policymakers, educators, and interested observers met at the Brookings Institution in Washington, D.C., to analyze a relatively new phenomenon in American education: national standards and assessments. The discussion devoted to the likely problems of national standards was timely and apt, because only a few weeks earlier Congress had enacted Goals 2000: Educate America Act, the Clinton administration's program to create state and national education standards. However, discussion devoted to the fate of national testing was hortatory and admonitory, because both the Clinton administration and Congress had rejected national testing.

The symposium, sponsored by the Brown Center on Education Policy at the Brookings Institution, was made possible by the generosity of The Pew Charitable Trusts. It brought together several of those who had played a leading role in the national debate about standards and assessments. The intention of the symposium was not to endorse a course of action but to reflect on the new legislation.

The conference on which this book is based would not have taken place without the enthusiastic support of Henry J. Aaron, Thomas E. Mann, and Bruce K. MacLaury of the Brookings Institution. The book would not have become a reality without the persistence and support of Anita G. Whitlock. Both owe their existence to the sponsorship of the Brown Center on Education Policy at the Brookings Institution and The Pew Charitable Trusts.

Diane Ravitch

Contents

Contributors

Chester E. Finn, Jr., is the John M. Olin Fellow at the Hudson Institute in Washington, D.C.

Daniel M. Koretz is a resident scholar with the RAND Institute on Education and Training who has conducted extensive research on issues related to educational assessment and reform.

Katherine J. Nolan is at the Learning Research and Development Center at the University of Pittsburgh.

Andrew C. Porter is professor of educational psychology and director of the Wisconsin Center for Education Research at the University of Wisconsin.

Diane Ravitch is a senior research scholar at New York University and a nonresident senior fellow at the Brookings Institution.

Lauren B. Resnick is professor of psychology at the University of Pittsburgh, where she directs the Learning Research and Development Center, and is also director of the New Standards Project.

Roy Romer is the governor of Colorado.

Albert Shanker is the president of the American Federation of Teachers.

Theodore R. Sizer is Walter H. Annenberg Professor of Education at Brown University and chair of the Coalition of Essential Schools.

Marshall S. Smith is the undersecretary of the U.S. Department of Education.

Donald M. Stewart is the president of the College Board.

Introduction

In 1975 Americans learned that scores on the nation's most widely used college entrance examination (the Scholastic Aptitude Test—or SAT) had been declining for more than a decade. This revelation was followed by a flurry of studies and reports describing the poor performance of American students and the wide gaps between high and low achievers. The most celebrated report was *A Nation at Risk,* issued in 1983 by the National Commission on Excellence in Education. Its documentation of poor performance, low expectations, and complacency set off a loud alarm about the condition of elementary and secondary education and inspired many states to raise their graduation requirements and to investigate additional ways of improving student achievement.

In 1994, eleven years after the release of *A Nation at Risk,* Congress passed Goals 2000: Educate America Act, which was intended to lay the groundwork for development of state and national standards in education. Six weeks after the passage of Goals 2000, a conference was held at the Brookings Institution to debate the significance of the new law. The participants assumed that Goals 2000 would be implemented as written, and the debate about its implications for the future was lively, with strong voices on different sides of the issues. No one at the symposium anticipated that the Republican party would gain control of Congress as a result of the November 1994 election. The new Congress made clear its intention to rewrite Goals 2000 to minimize federal intrusion into state and local control of schools. Some members of Congress wanted to repeal it altogether. Others wanted only to eliminate any federal authority to tell states what to teach. The law had not been rewritten at the time of publication of this volume.

Whether Goals 2000 is repealed or revised, the underlying issues persist. Although exceptions exist, student performance remains distressingly poor; standards and expectations are too low; most states, using money supplied under Goals 2000, are developing new content and performance standards; few states or school districts have assessments that are tied to high standards; most American parents do not know whether their children are getting a good education. These are the reasons that the idea of standards and assessments became an important item on the national agenda; and these are the reasons that the underlying issues cannot be avoided regardless of how Congress changes the legislation passed in 1994.

School reform in the United States has been a century-long preoccupation, and cynics might have discounted the state-level reforms of the 1980s as another go-round in a perennial exercise. But educational improvement in the late twentieth century became a necessity, not a luxury, in view of changes in the national economy that narrowed economic opportunity for poorly educated workers. Recognizing that the future health of their state and the nation depended on improving education, many governors, educators, business leaders, and other citizens became actively involved in efforts to improve the quality of American education. Heightened concern about education eventually became a national issue, and in the 1988 presidential campaign, candidate George Bush promised to be "the education president." In 1989 President Bush convened a meeting in Charlottesville, Virginia, at which he and the nation's governors agreed to establish national education goals. A few months later, after extensive consultations with the governors (including Bill Clinton of Arkansas), President Bush announced six goals for the year 2000:

1. All children in American will start school ready to learn.

2. The high school graduation rate will increase to at least 90 percent.

3. American students will leave grades four, eight, and twelve having demonstrated competency in challenging subject matter including English, mathematics, science, history, and geography; and every school in America will ensure that all students learn to use their minds well, so they may be prepared for responsible citizenship, further learning, and productive employment in the modern economy.

4. U.S. students will be first in the world in science and mathematics achievement.

5. Every adult American will be literate and possess the knowledge and skills necessary to compete in a global economy and exercise the rights and responsibilities of citizenship.

6. Every school in America will be free of drugs and violence and will offer a safe, disciplined environment conducive to learning.[1]

Soon after the promulgation of the national goals, the National Education Goals Panel was created, consisting of governors and representatives of the administration; its purpose was to monitor the nation's progress toward the goals.

While the goals were comprehensive in their reach, they established a clear focus on improving educational achievement. The specific language of goals three and four suggested the need for some kind of standards and assessments. In the absence of standards, how would "challenging subject matter" be defined? In the absence of assessments, how could students demonstrate mastery? How would anyone know whether these goals had been reached unless broad agreement existed on what was to be learned and how well it was to be learned?

At an abstract level, a compelling case can be made for national standards and national assessments, because they are a way of establishing what needs to be taught and learned and whether progress is being made. But manifold political and educational problems arise when moving from theory to implementation: Who would establish the standards? What process would ensure that national standards would be high? Who would write the tests? Would they be compulsory or voluntary? Should test results be used to determine graduation or college admission? What consequences, if any, should follow for students who did not meet national standards? Should students be held accountable for their academic performance if their schools do not provide equal opportunity to learn? Will the expansion of the federal role in education intrude upon the authority over education normally exercised by state and local governments?

Historically, with few exceptions, elementary and secondary education has been a state and local function. Although the role of the federal government has expanded substantially in recent decades, less than 10 percent of the cost of public schooling is covered by federal funding. While many small federal programs for the schools exist, the primary beneficiaries of federal support have been disadvantaged and handicapped children. In matters of curriculum, the federal role has been negligible, by law and common agreement. Although many other nations have a national curriculum and national testing, education in the United States respects the principle of federalism; states have the primary responsibility for what is taught and tested in schools. Only on rare occasions has the federal government offered (not mandated) funds for strategically important subject matter such as science, mathematics, and foreign languages. And federal support for educational testing has been limited to the National Assessment of Educational Progress, which since 1970 has tested national samples of students in different subject areas to chart the progress and condition of American education.

The movement to develop national standards and national tests started during the Bush administration. The Republican party had been traditionally reluctant to expand the federal role in education; by contrast, the Democrats saw the federal government as the primary guarantor of equity for disadvantaged populations, not as a proponent of high academic standards. Although public opinion polls showed large majorities of the public favoring national standards and a national test, political forces on the right and left were deeply divided and uneasy. Republicans worried about the dangers of ideological and political manipulation by federal bureaucrats in charge of standards and testing. Democrats were wary of a cause championed by a Republican president, and civil rights organizations feared that minority students would earn low scores on national tests and that the results of such tests would narrow educational and economic opportunities for those students. In addition, the politically potent National Education Association had deep misgivings about standards and assessments as a reform strategy.

A year after the promulgation of the national education goals, President Bush enlisted as his secretary of education the former governor of Tennessee, Lamar Alexander, who had made education reform the keystone of his plans for economic growth. Alexander and his deputy secretary, David Kearns, devised the AMERICA 2000 strategy to advance the national goals. It was designed to promote ground-level, populist education reforms, not an enlargement of the federal role. As part of AMERICA 2000, local leaders in thousands of communities organized to pursue the goals; a private entity, the New American Schools Development Corporation, was created to sponsor a design competition for "break-the-mold" schools; parental choice of schools—public and nonpublic—was encouraged; and support was pledged for voluntary national standards and national tests.

To explore the feasibility of national standards and national tests, the Bush administration persuaded Congress to establish the National Council on Education Standards and Testing. This bipartisan body, cochaired by Governor Roy Romer of Colorado and Governor Carroll

A. Campbell, Jr., of South Carolina (who also cochaired the National Education Goals Panel), issued a report early in 1992, which endorsed national standards and testing in accordance with the following principles:

—Standards must reflect high expectations, not expectations of minimal competency.

—Standards must provide focus, not become a national curriculum.

—Standards must be national, not federal.

—Standards must be voluntary, not mandated by the federal government.

—Standards must be dynamic, not static.[2]

—Assessments must be multiple, not a single national test; assessments would be linked to common national standards, but they would be controlled by individual states or groups of states.

—Assessments must be voluntary, not mandatory; state participation in the national system of assessments would be voluntary.

—Assessments must evolve over time but remain aligned with national content and performance standards.[3]

The panel identified three types of standards: national content standards (what children are taught); national performance standards (the level of performance that is considered "good enough"); and school delivery standards (the capacity of schools and school systems to provide equal opportunity for students to reach high standards). School delivery standards are called opportunity-to-learn standards (OTL) in Goals 2000.

During the last full year of the Bush administration—a presidential election year—no education legislation was enacted. However, the U.S. Department of Education (in collaboration with the National Endowment for the Humanities and other federal agencies) made grants to consortia of scholars, teachers, and others to develop voluntary national content standards in science, history, geography, the arts, civics, English, and foreign languages.[4] Each group was expected to engage in a broad and inclusive consensus process to determine what students in each field should know and be able to do at various stages of their schooling. Standards in mathematics had already been developed by the National Council of Teachers of Mathematics.

During the 1992 presidential campaign, candidate Bill Clinton advocated the development of high standards and a meaningful examination system for the nation. After the election, President Clinton's

Department of Education—led by former governor Richard W. Riley of South Carolina, who had won a national reputation for his education reforms—submitted Goals 2000. The legislation was enacted in March 1994.

Goals 2000 formally authorized the National Education Goals Panel and codified the national education goals, adding two new goals—one on parent participation and another on teacher training. The act created a new federal agency, the National Education Standards and Improvement Council (NESIC), which was to be responsible for certifying voluntary national content and performance standards; voluntary national opportunity-to-learn standards; and state standards for content, performance, and opportunity-to-learn, as well as state assessments. NESIC was supposed to ensure that national standards "are internationally competitive and comparable to the best in the world" and that state standards "are comparable or higher in rigor and quality" to the national standards. By law, NESIC was to be representative in terms of race, ethnicity, gender, and disability characteristics, and at least one-third of its nineteen members were to have experience in dealing with the needs of low-income, minority, limited-English-speaking, and handicapped children.

Goals 2000 also established a grant program to enable states to design their own reform plans, including content, performance, and OTL standards, as well as assessments. The law made no provision for national testing and prohibited the use of federally funded state tests for any decisions affecting students, such as promotion or graduation. Under the law, the bipartisan National Education Goals Panel would review NESIC's decisions and could overturn them by a two-thirds majority. Also, the secretary of education was authorized to award grants to one or more consortia to develop voluntary national opportunity-to-learn standards, which included the quality and availability of curricula, instructional materials, technologies, staff, teacher-training programs, buildings, libraries, laboratories, and other resources.

After the Republican party won control of Congress in 1994, criticism of Goals 2000 centered on NESIC and OTL standards. Critics saw NESIC as a national school board, which would have the power to interfere with state curricula. OTL standards had always been the most controversial aspect of Goals 2000. When the legislation was debated, both Democratic and Republican governors worried that OTL standards would become the basis for lawsuits, costly regulations, unfunded federal mandates, and other intrusions into the delivery of education.

Even after passage of Goals 2000, the debate about standards and assessments clearly was far from over. Some educators worried whether national standards would narrow the curriculum to academic subjects and whether they diverted attention from pressing social issues. Others worried that NESIC might endorse low standards to achieve consensus, impose a coercive and politically biased national curriculum, and intrude into issues that belonged to the local and state levels. After the 1994 elections, when it appeared that NESIC would be eliminated, supporters of standards worried how states would determine whether their standards were high enough and how they compared to standards in other states and nations. Even without NESIC, there will still be a need for a public agency to review state and national standards and comment on their quality. The National Education Goals Panel, bipartisan and dominated by governors, is likely to assume this function on an advisory basis, without the power to "certify" standards.

Other kinds of controversies were emerging in various states and communities, in large part because the changes promised by Goals 2000 were so little understood and so little discussed outside of Washington, D.C. In several states, angry partisans campaigned against "outcome-based education" (OBE), which they saw not as academic standards but as behavioral and attitudinal objectives imposed on their children by education bureaucrats. In some communities, the critics of OBE rejected the proposition that all children can learn, on grounds that the purpose was to dumb down the curriculum and hold back the brightest children until the slowest ones catch up with them. The anti–OBE forces also criticized performance assessment, which they saw as part of a plot to eliminate any real standards by getting rid of objective, standardized tests. The attacks on OBE often were broadened into critiques of all efforts to set standards or to deviate from multiple-choice tests. Some of these fears—though not all of them— stem from the paucity of public discussion about the issues. Although five years passed between the national education summit in 1989 and passage of Goals 2000 in 1994, relatively little attention was paid in the press or the mass media to the proposed changes. The discussions in the nation's capital during that time had direct bearing on the relationships among the federal, state, and local governments on education issues, but the press was not much interested and the public was largely unaware of what was happening. Under the circumstances, misinformation, misunderstanding, and fear easily fed on each other.

Participants in the Brookings symposium disagreed on many central issues regarding the value of national standards and assessments. On one point, though, they did agree: the importance of a public dialogue about these issues. An ongoing commitment to debate and discussion, conducted in a spirit of civility, is vital to achieve the level of public understanding that is needed for the improvement of education.

NOTES

1. National Education Goals Panel, *Building a Nation of Learners* (Washington, 1991), p. ix.

2. National Council on Education Standards and Testing, *Raising Standards in American Education* (Washington, 1991), p. 3.

3. National Council on Education Standards and Testing, *Raising Standards in American Education*, p. 15.

4. In 1994 the Department of Education cut off funding to the English standards project, citing its lack of progress.

MARSHALL S. SMITH

Education Reform in America's Public Schools: The Clinton Agenda

During 1994, the Clinton administration's K-12 education reform legislation successfully passed the 103d Congress with bipartisan majorities, and it is now being actively implemented by the Department of Education. On November 8, 1994, shortly after the last piece of legislation was signed into law, the nation took a turn to the right, and the Republican party took control of the 104th Congress. Among the items on the agenda of some Republican leaders is the elimination or redesign of the Department of Education and of much of the education legislation overwhelmingly passed by the previous Congress.

This chapter reviews the logic and the research behind the administration's reforms, describes the reform legislation, and concludes with some observations about the future of standards-based reform.[1]

CONTEXT FOR THE CLINTON AGENDA

The need for American students to learn more demanding content and skills became increasingly clear in the 1980s. The United States faces great challenges: internally, by the need to maintain a strong democracy in a complex and diverse society; externally, by a competitive economic environment that will be dominated by high-skill jobs. Success will depend in substantial part on the caacity of all citizens to thoughtfully and knowledgeably engage in helping to meet the nation's challenges.

In response to these challenges, U.S. education entered an unprecedented period of reform. Research conducted since the mid-1970s has provided new understandings about ways to improve teaching and learning, the curriculum, educational governance, and assessment. During the 1980s many states passed and implemented ambitious education reform legislation. At the local level, thousands of school districts tried many different strategies to improve performance. Public schools, meanwhile, worked to implement the many reforms stimulated by local, state, and federal governments and by education innovators, as well as to stay abreast of new research.

Although the reforms did not meet the expectations of the public and the critics of American public education, it was clear by 1992 that they had had significant success. Dropout rates were at their lowest level ever, while mathematics and science scores reached their highest. Moreover, our high school students regularly take more rigorous academic courses, and the number of students taking and passing Advanced Placement courses has increased manyfold since 1980.[2]

Despite this success and the fact that our finest schools and students can compete with the best in the world, however, international comparisons of educational achievement indicate that the United States lags behind many countries in both educational excellence and equality.[3]

The Goals 2000: Educate America Act (P.L. 103-227), and the reauthorization of the Elementary and Secondary Education Act of 1965 (ESEA), represent the attempt of the Clinton administration to use the new knowledge and to help sustain the enthusiasm, energy, and success of the 1980 reforms. The legislation is designed to support the efforts of state and local governments and schools to achieve the goal of higher academic achievement for *all* students. It builds on our understanding that *all* children can learn to higher levels than we have previously thought possible and reinforces the emerging movement at the state and local level to define challenging content and performance standards to guide education reform. Finally, the legislation removes much of the burdensome regulatory structure of federal involvement in K-12 schooling, to help provide schools the flexibility they need to effectively teach all their students.[4]

CORE PRINCIPLES OF THE ADMINISTRATION'S EDUCATION PROPOSALS

Four core principles guided the development of the legislation.

Clear and Challenging Academic Standards for All Students

State content and performance standards that establish challenging academic expectations for *all* students are at the heart of the administration's systemic reform strategy. Content standards (sometimes

FIGURE 1. *Content Standards*

The following is drawn from the National Council of Teachers of Mathematics (NCTM) standards for mathematics for grades nine through twelve. At each of three grade spans (one to four, five to eight, nine to twelve), the NCTM standards set out clear expectations for what students should know and be able to do in mathematics.

In grades five to eight, the mathematics curriculum should include the study of the geometry of one, two, and three dimensions in a variety of situations so that students can

- **identify, describe, compare, and classify geometric figures;**
- **visualize and represent geometric figures with special attention to developing spatial sense;**
- **explore transformations of geometric figures;**
- **represent and solve problems using geometric models;**
- **understand and apply geometric properties and relationships; and**
- **develop an appreciation of geometry as a means of describing the physical world.**

NCTM created about thirteen similar standards for three grade clusters (kindergarten to four, five to eight, nine to twelve); that is, forty standards, plus explanations and sample learning activities. NCTM saw the standards as "a coherent vision of what it means to be mathematically literate." They were designed to be used to "guide the revision of the school mathematics curriculum" and assessment.

---

called "curriculum frameworks") set out what all students should know and be able to do in the core academic areas; performance standards provide clear targets for expected levels of student accomplishment (see figures 1 and 2 for examples of content and performance standards). While content and performance standards alone cannot reform schools, they can establish a core set of substantive expectations for all students and, therefore, act as a guide to bring rigor and focus to every school and classroom.

The administration's reforms are designed to support and invigorate a movement toward challenging and collectively agreed upon state standards, a movement that has gained substantial momentum

FIGURE 2. *Performance Standards*

The following is an example of a performance standard and a sample student work drawn from the Kentucky performance assessment.

As part of the 1991-92 KIRIS Assessment, each eighth grader in Kentucky responded to three open-ended questions in reading, mathematics, science. and social studies. Responses were assessed as demonstrating distinguished, proficient, apprentice, or novice performance. For example, in science, the question was asked: "How would life and other conditions on earth be different if all bacteria and fungi became extinct? Explain the changes that might occur and give as much detail as possible." The response below was assessed as "distinguished" performance in eighth grade.

Though extremely minute, bacteria and fungi have an enormous role in life on Earth. Without them, many changes would occur. Bacteria break down dead organic matter so it will decay. If bacteria and fungi became extinct, the dead animals would never decompose. Instead, they would keep accumulating until there would be no room for humans to live. This would also cause serious environmental problems. The build-up of the dead organisms would create poor living conditions, not to mention the sickening smell. Decayed organic matter fertilizes the soil so that plants can grow. If the bacteria did not cause decay, the plants could not grow. If plants did not grow, humans would be left without a food source. Food chains of every kind would be upset without the help of bacteria and fungi. Also, oxygen could not be produced if there were no plants. Some bacteria change the nitrogen in the air to a form that plants can use. Again, the lack of bacteria would be a hinderance to plant growth. Fungi and bacteria also cause and spread diseases. With the extinction of bacteria and fungi, many common diseases today may become extinct. Though, this would seem like a good change, it could also be a problem. If no animal or human contracted a disease, the world would become overpopulated. In turn, a food shortage would occur. Life would be even more difficult without the diseases. Therefore, this world would certainly be harmed by the extinction of bacteria and fungi.

The student at the distinguished level presents an articulate, thorough, and complete response to each question, using concise and precise analyses. The response clearly shows an understanding of scientific thought processes and procedures, the application of the same, and an extension beyond the expected achievement for a student at this grade level.

since the late 1980s. A recent *Education Week* review reports that about forty-five states have developed or are developing content standards in a number of academic areas; it appears from this report that by 1996 almost all states will have embarked on the process.[5]

Content standards should provide guidance about the knowledge and skills that all children should be given the opportunity to learn. They should establish clear goals for learning—outlining expectations to be achieved by, for example, fourth, eighth and twelfth grades. To be effective, the standards should be detailed enough to provide guidance for assessments and curriculum materials but not so fine-grained as to prescribe the specific curricula and pedagogy for schools. By setting out core content expectations over three- or four-year blocks of time, for example, schools would have the flexibility to design their curricula to best meet the needs of their students.

In addition, the standards must be challenging. They should build on our new understandings about teaching and the capacity of all students to learn, and they should be dynamic, open to change as new knowledge is obtained. If they fall short of these criteria, as did many state minimum competency requirements in the 1970s, the reforms will surely fail.

States have not been the only organizations developing education standards. At the national level, the National Council of Teachers of Mathematics, after a massive effort involving a large number of teachers and mathematicians, produced in 1989 an exemplary set of content standards for K-12 mathematics, which have served as a model for many states (see figure 1). Since then, a number of other national professional groups have begun developing content standards for their academic areas. The Clinton administration has supported the development of some of these standards with the sole intent of providing useful exemplars for states as they establish their standards.[6] Believing that the locus for reform should be within states, the administration explicitly rejected the idea of common national standards that would be required of all states.

Federal, State, and Local Policies to Support Teaching and Learning

If the core academic purpose of education is to provide *all* students with the opportunity to achieve to higher standards, the energy and activities of the system ought to be focused on furthering this goal.

Moreover, resources should be directed in support of the teachers and schools responsible for ensuring that students learn to the state standards. Federal, state, and local policies should all be pedaling in the same direction. Too often in American schools, resource decisions are not guided by clear academic goals, a condition that can lead to inefficiency and ineffectiveness.

Curriculum materials that support learning the standards ought to be available to teachers and schools. Assessments of student achievement ought to aligned with the content standards so that they provide information about the success of students in reaching the standards and so that students and schools that have worked hard to reach higher standards are rewarded.

Most important, teachers must be prepared to teach to the standards. The new standards-based reforms should ask much of teachers. The standards will draw from research conducted since the mid-1970s that indicates that students can learn far more challenging content and skills than they have in the past, if effectively taught by knowledgeable teachers. New information also exists about effective pedagogy, and many teachers will have to learn both new content and new ways of teaching to be successful.[7]

New demands on teachers also point to the need for rigorous strategies for reforming preservice teacher training, teacher licensing, and certification assessments and decisions. Teacher preservice training and professional development should be concentrated on preparing new teachers to help all students achieve to the standards.

Ultimately, all levels of the education system, including schools, should have the capacity to operate in a coherent and creative manner. However, this condition is rare in the highly fragmented and often bureaucratic policy environment of American schooling.[8]

Local Flexibility and Responsibility

A coherent system can help provide the sustained support required for large numbers of schools to generate "bottom-up reforms" that can enable all students to meet challenging state standards. To make this work, however, teachers and schools should have the authority and responsibility to design the school day, the curriculum, sequencing, instructional strategies, and other teaching and learning activities within the school. Teachers must be able to use the best professional knowledge available, to experiment with promising ideas, and to adjust to individual, community, and cultural differences.

To accomplish this, all levels of government should steer away from top-down micromanagement. Federal and state governments can nurture local flexibility and responsibility by limiting both the number and requirements of categorical programs to only the essential, reducing regulations and paperwork, creating positive incentives, offering waivers, and providing ongoing and substantive technical assistance. Many local education agencies could direct a greater level of their resources toward direct support of teaching and learning in the schools and help schools create environments more conducive to teacher-generated improvement.

Ultimately, for standards-based reform to work, teachers must be engaged; study after study documents the need to involve teachers continually in the process of developing and implementing reforms.[9] This means, for example, approaching teachers as knowledgeable participants in the process of devising standards and developing curricula and assessments based on the standards. And it means giving teachers a full voice in the development of schoolwide reform plans and the opportunity to participate in networks and other professional activities.

Accountability and Improvement

The fourth principle for widespread and effective educational reform is a useful system of accountability and improvement. In my view, effective reform should emphasize two aspects of this component—one formal, the other informal. In a formal accountability system, students, institutions (schools, districts), or both might be held responsible (by districts and states, for example) for continuous improvement toward meeting performance standards. Corrective steps, rewards, and sanctions based on performance could be required.

Informal accountability relies not on an external mechanism for ensuring performance, but on ongoing information and self-generated professional responsibility for continuous school and student improvement. This approach recognizes that external accountability is only one of many ways to motivate people and often not the most successful.

Both aspects of accountability depend to some extent on the systems of assessment. Currently, typical state and district assessment systems are based on norm-referenced, short-answer tests that are often substantially unrelated to the curricula of the schools. The kinds of assessments envisioned in the standards-based reforms would be aligned with the curriculum since both the curriculum and the assessments will be aligned with the content standards. They also would be richer in content and character, involving multiple strategies for measuring student achievement, including student work in portfolios, performance assessments, and short-answer questions.

Because the new assessments will be aligned with the curricula, they would help provide a legitimate basis for a formal accountability system to assess the progress of both students and the schools in reaching the standards.[10] An assessment system that is aligned with the curricula would reward the hard work of students and teachers, while one that is essentially independent of the curricula will not. The new assessments also should provide the basis for an informal accountability system that feeds back rich and useful information for school administrators, teachers, and the public to use to continuously improve school programs.

A third accountability strategy is parental choice. Here the administration's strategy supports public school choice in its current forms and through new mechanisms such as "charter schools."

ADMINISTRATION STRATEGIES

The Clinton administration's major strategies to transform these principles into policy are contained in Goals 2000 and the closely linked Improving America's Schools Act, which reauthorized the Elementary and Secondary Education Act.

Goals 2000

Goals 2000 was enacted in March 1994 with bipartisan congressional support, as well as the backing of the major business, education, and labor groups in the nation. The law establishes a framework for the federal government to support state and local reforms focused on improving the academic achievement of all students.

The Goals 2000 legislation breaks new ground for the federal government. Legislation before Goals 2000 focused either on categorical groups of students such as the disabled, the limited-English proficient, or low-achieving students in high-poverty schools, or on targeted areas such as vocational education or "drug-free schools," or on general aid. Never before has the federal government enacted legislation designed to help states and school districts to upgrade the quality of the core academic program for _all_ students. This strategy allows the federal government to pursue the legitimate national interest of helping to improve America's schools while simultaneously respecting traditions of control over education by state and local governments.

The Goals 2000 legislation creates a national component that is administered entirely independently of the Department of Education and a grant program to stimulate state and local reform that is administered by the department.

The National Component. Title I of the legislation sets out eight national education goals. The goals, six developed in 1990 under the leadership of President George Bush and the nation's governors and two added by the 103d Congress, establish ambitious targets for U.S. education.[11]

Title II of the legislation establishes in law the National Education Goals Panel (NEGP) and the National Education Standards and Improvement Council (NESIC). These were intended to be tiny, federally funded, independent agencies, with no necessary administrative or policy relationship to the U.S. Department of Education. At the time of passage, the administration and lawmakers had great hopes for the potential of each to play an important national educational and leadership role in support of state and local reform.

NEGP was originally created in 1990 by agreement of the president and the governors as a unique bipartisan body of state and federal officials, to help build national consensus for educational improvement and to monitor and report on progress toward achieving the national education goals. The panel meets regularly and has the authority to hold hearings, commission studies and reviews, and publish and disseminate reports, including a yearly report that was initiated in 1991 on the nation's progress toward meeting the national goals. In its early years NEGP played an active role in advocating standards-based education reform. It continues to carry out this role, although it is fair to say that NEGP is now, in mid-1995, searching for a clear strategy to accomplish its legislative purposes.

NESIC, intended to be an even more broadly based, bipartisan body, is a somewhat different story. NESIC was authorized by Congress as a successor to the National Council on Education Standards and Testing, an earlier congressionally mandated bipartisan body that in 1992 recommended standards-based state reforms and the development of *voluntary* national standards for the various academic areas.[12] The responsibility of the new council, as stated in the legislation, is to promote high-quality standards and assessments throughout the U.S. education system by stimulating the development of and certifying voluntary national standards that would serve as "world class" examples for states developing their own standards and, upon state request, certifying state standards and assessments that are *voluntarily* submitted by the states, if the state standards are comparable in quality to the voluntary national standards and if the assessments are aligned with state standards that have been previously certified by NESIC.

Because its purposes would be focused on standards and assessments, NESIC was seen by some to be integral to the reform effort. Yet even as the legislation passed, the eventual importance of the body was uncertain, for by statute the council has no necessary relationship to the reforms going on in the states and no direct influence on the operation of the Department of Education.[13]

The legislation makes clear that the voluntary national standards that NESIC would certify are truly voluntary. States would not have to adopt them. States would not have to base their content standards or curriculum frameworks on the voluntary national standards; states would not have to submit their standards to NESIC for certification. In effect, states could safely ignore NESIC and the voluntary national standards. The Goals 2000 statute expressly bans any imposition of national standards of any sort, voluntary or otherwise.

The ambiguity of NESIC's role in relationship to the reforms has contributed to the probable demise of the council. Three views of NESIC have surfaced over the past year, stimulated by the reports of at least three different study groups of education experts. The first is a minimalist one that would have the council go quietly about its business of deciding what standards and assessments to certify in a relatively technical manner. This role would seem to accomplish little beyond meeting the letter of the statutory mandates. A second view is that NESIC would carry out its certification functions and also take on an educational role. In this expanded capacity, NESIC, through public forums and hearings, would help the nation explore the issues of "what all students should know and be able to do" and of "what it will take for all students to succeed to the performance standards that NESIC certifies." To fulfill this more ambitious role, NESIC would have as members thoughtful and respected citizens and would operate as a public education mechanism, to consider, in Whitehead's words, "the aims of education."

A third and more alarmist view is that NESIC could expand on the educational role and become, in effect, a politically appointed "national school board" that could potentially exceed legislative intent in its influence over curricular and other educational decisions that are traditionally vested in state and local authorities. The specter of this view, which was widely circulated by conservative groups even though there was no legislative basis for it, and the delay by Congress in developing its nominations for appointment to the council, led over the last months of 1994 and early months of 1995 to a growing opposition to NESIC. As of late July 1995, the president had not appointed the members of NESIC, the goals panel had indicated that it believed that NESIC is not necessary, there were bills pending in both the House and the Senate that would eliminate the authorization for the council, and the funding for NESIC for 1995 had been rescinded by Congress. Few believe that NESIC will ever exist.

The lack of a clear strategy for the goals panel and NESIC's troubles suggest to some that the national movement toward standards-based reforms is endangered. The facts, however, seem to belie this concern. National support for the standards movement has been as much, if not more, a product of nonfederal national organizations than of the federal government. Professional science organizations, such as the National Academy of Sciences and the American Association for the Advancement of Science, similar organizations reflecting other academic discipline areas, most of the core national education associations, the National Governors' Association, national business groups such as the Business Roundtable and the National Alliance of Business, labor unions, and a wide variety of other organizations such as the Council for Basic Education and the New Standards Project have supported both legislative and private activities directed at advancing state reforms based on more challenging standards for all students. Over the long run the sustained interest and support of these organizations is far more important to the standards movement than the presence and efforts of federally created councils.

The State Component. Support for state and local education improvement is the core of Goals 2000. Title III of the new act provides grants to states for planning and implementing statewide reform focused on helping all students achieve to challenging academic standards. Just as involvement with NESIC would be entirely voluntary for states, so is seeking and using funds under Title III. No provision in the act applies to states that do not request and receive funding from Goals 2000.

If a state does receive funds from Goals 2000, it may use a portion for statewide reform efforts, while directing the bulk of the resources through grants to school districts for planning and implementing their reforms. Although the funds from Goals 2000 are tiny compared with state and local school budgets, they provide unencumbered resources that can help spur creativity and positive change.

For up to two years, a state may receive its share of the funding simply by completing a short four-page application indicating how it will go about planning for reform. After two years, the state must have an approved reform plan to receive further funding. In recognition that many states were well under way toward planning and implementing standards-based reforms when Goals 2000 was enacted, the legislation allows the secretary of education to approve preexisting planning structures and plans that meet the spirit of the law as satisfying the act's planning and participation requirements.

To take part in Goals 2000, states and school districts by law are asked to establish a broad participatory process that involves parents and other local community representatives in planning, developing, and implementing strategies for reform of the educational system. In addition, the state plan is expected to include information about how the state has established or would establish challenging state content and performance standards for all students in the core academic areas and state assessments that are aligned with the state standards. It would also show how its professional development and other reform strategies support *all* students learning to higher standards and how it is "promoting comprehensive, bottom-up systemic reform in communities, local education agencies, and schools through provision of overall local flexibility and waivers from state rules and regulations."

A state submits its improvement plan to the secretary. Although the secretary has the responsibility of approving plans, endorsement comes only after substantive peer review of the plans by teachers, members of state and local educational agencies, and the broader educational community. Peer reviews involve both a review of submitted materials and a site visit to the state.

This process is substantially different from the one that has been used to approve other federal formula grants to states, and it signals an important change in approach by the Clinton administration. The new emphasis is on professional judgment, with a focus on substantive matters and outcomes, instead of on compliance with procedures and rules. The use of peer reviews to assess state plans helps establish the fundamental idea that professional judgment and expertise are critical to all aspects of this reform. It may also help create a national network of education professionals and others knowledgeable about the reforms.

Goals 2000 contains another important new provision designed to support local and state reform and flexibility. For the first time in the history of the department, the secretary has a broad waiver authority that, with a few specific exceptions, allows him to waive almost any statutory or regulatory requirement of the six largest federal grant programs that provide resources for K-12 education, if the requirement impedes school improvement activities and if the state agrees to waive similar requirements in state law.

Finally, no regulations have been or will be issued for Goals 2000. Instead, the department has provided general guidance, with an emphasis on examples and demonstrations of good practice, support for technical assistance, and applied research and development. As part of this effort, the department is refocusing its monitoring and assistance efforts to directly support the successful implementation of the state and local reform strategies included in the Goals 2000 improvement plans.

Goals 2000 has been well received by most states. By May 1994, shortly after the passage of the bill, more than thirty states had applied for their first-year funding and applications were expected from almost all of the rest.

By July 1995, participation in Goals 2000 was up to forty-eight states, as well as the District of Columbia, Puerto Rico, and eight territories. Moreover, fourteen states have submitted full plans and five have been fully approved. The department expects approximately two more plans to be submitted by the end of the summer. The fiscal year 1995 appropriation is approximately $400 million, a fourfold increase over the $100 million appropriation in 1994.

Implementation of Goals 2000, however, has not been as smooth as these numbers appear to indicate. In many states there has been significant political and ideological opposition to participation in the act. Indeed, Goals 2000 has become a "lightning rod" for antagonism toward education reform in some states. At the risk of oversimplification, the opposition seems to stem from four overlapping sources: traditions of local control in states such as Iowa and New Hampshire; a belief by various groups that oppose federal involvement in education that Goals 2000 will bring the teaching of "progressive values" that they disapprove of; a belief by some that the reform's emphasis on challenging content and higher order thinking will deemphasize learning "the basics;" and a contrary belief that a goal of high standards for all will ultimately result in mediocre expectations for all.

At the state level, these concerns have resulted in delays in applications for Goals 2000 funds and in two cases no application at all. More important, they have led to delays in developing state and local reform efforts. At the federal level, the new Congress proposed cuts in the 1995 Goals 2000 appropriations in its large rescission bill but achieved them in only the national program part of the act. The state-level appropriation stayed largely intact. Future appropriations, however, are even more in jeopardy.

The administration's response to the opposition has been to focus its efforts on resolving concerns at the state and local levels. The intent has been to honor the traditions of the states and the progress that they have made toward comprehensive improvement while simultaneously adhering to the intent of the legislation to promote challenging standards and opportunities for all students.

ESEA Reauthorization: The Improving America's Schools Act

The preamble of Goals 2000 states that the act provides "a framework for the reauthorization of all Federal education programs" by, in essence, supporting state and local reform. The ESEA, with approximately $10 billion in annual appropriations, is the major federal K-12 legislation. The reauthorization of the ESEA passed Congress in the closing moments of the 103d Congress. The new law took effect on July 1, 1995.

Throughout the administration's reauthorization proposal (and remaining in the final version of the legislation), the emphasis is on designing federal programs to support state and district reform efforts.

Instead of viewing ESEA as a set of discrete and separate federal programs, the reauthorization focuses squarely on strengthening the teaching and learning needed to enable all students to reach high state standards.

The new legislation reflects the four principles set out earlier. First, in keeping with the purposes of the ESEA since its inception in 1965, the reauthorization aims the great majority of ESEA resources at supporting efforts to improve teaching and learning for the neediest students. The difference in this reauthorization is that the focus is on enhanced opportunities for these students to learn to the *same* challenging standards as other, more advantaged students in their districts and states.

The best known program and the largest by far, Title I (formerly Chapter 1), at an appropriation in fiscal year 1995 of approximately $6.5 billion, serves as an example. The approach also is applied to the programs for limited-English proficient, migrant, neglected and delinquent, and homeless students.

Title I is designed to help improve the academic success of low-achieving students in high-poverty schools. The reauthorization proposal introduced by the Clinton administration and passed by Congress calls for schools in states that have challenging content and performance standards for all children to focus their Title I instruction on bringing their students to meet those standards. The intent is to eliminate dual curricula—a challenging one for the affluent areas and a diluted, remedial one for inner cities and poor rural areas. Funds from the new Title I are intended to support efforts of high-poverty schools to enrich their curriculum and instruction to enable disadvantaged children to learn basic skills and then progress well beyond them to meet more challenging standards.

The emphasis on integrating Title I instructional services with the core curriculum exists throughout the newly reauthorized program. An expansion of the schoolwide program approach will allow many high-poverty schools to coordinate their federal and state categorical programs with the core curriculum of the school and will open opportunities for all children in the schools to achieve to high standards. In non-schoolwide programs, the reauthorization provisions are intended to discourage inappropriate Title I pull-out programs that isolate children in dead-end tracks and to encourage extended-time strategies and other targeted assistance based on research on teaching and learning.

The reauthorized ESEA eliminates special required testing of only

Title I students for placement and accountability purposes. The intent is that educational decisions, such as placement in Title I, will involve professional judgment informed by a thorough understanding of student work, not by single norm-referenced tests. For accountability purposes, Title I programs will rely on the same state assessment systems as used for all students to determine whether they are progressing toward the challenging state standards. Title I schools and districts will be held accountable for showing continuous improvement in student achievement on these assessments. Besides reducing the amount of testing, these changes should help link Title I programs to the broader state reforms.

The second principle is to have policies in support of the reforms. Title I and the other ESEA programs focused on the most needy meet this criterion. Two major new programs go beyond that to provide direct support for better teaching and learning in the schools. One of the programs helps to ensure that all teachers should be prepared to teach to the challenging state standards. The other recognizes that all schools must be safe and drug-free if they are to be effective learning environments.

The third principle is that districts and schools should have the flexibility, information, and knowledge they need to assist students to achieve to high academic standards. The reauthorization substantially increases the flexibility of schools and districts to administer federal programs. There are fewer reporting requirements, and a broad system of waivers is available to schools, districts, and states. A number of waiver requests under ESEA have already been submitted to the department and approved. Moreover, the department has aggressively reduced the regulatory burden. Of the major state grant programs in the new ESEA, only Part A of Title I will have any regulations, and those are required by law. The new, required regulations will be greatly reduced from the ones that previously existed.

The new ESEA also increases opportunities for applied research and demonstrations. Among the most important are authorities for developing and exploring uses of technology and for demonstrating and evaluating the effectiveness of charter schools. Over the longer run, the newly reauthorized Office of Educational Research and Improvement will strengthen and focus research efforts on providing support for the state reforms.

The accountability and continuous performance provisions in Title I, which meet the fourth principle, have already been mentioned.

In the past, the ESEA contained a collection of programs disconnected from each other and from educational improvement efforts in states, districts, and schools. In its new form, the intent is to have the ESEA use its $10 billion to strengthen state and local capacity to serve all students. As with almost all legislation, the enacted law is somewhat different from the administration's proposal. Nonetheless, the essential four principles have been retained. The hope is that the new law will have a powerful effect, one that will change the way federal programs operate at the state and local level, break down the existing categorical structure, and encourage state and local educators to take a broader, more integrated view of their efforts.

ENDURING ISSUES OF EDUCATION REFORM

Goals 2000 and the ESEA reauthorization are only a small part of the overall standards-based reform agenda in the United States. However, because they emphasize a comprehensive, systemic strategy, can affect all states and localities, and represent the federal position, they may have a substantially greater influence than their resources would typically merit. Nonetheless, the eventual effect of the federal effort will depend on the capacity and will of states and districts to manage and promote improvements in their schools. Throughout this process, debates and tensions will be evident, and large and small issues will have no neat or easy answers.

What, for example, are the characteristics of high-quality and effective content and performance standards? How can the long-term political will and attention necessary to put the reforms into practice be sustained? How can we "go to scale" in the professional development of more than 2 million teachers to prepare them to teach content and skills that they were not exposed to in school and in a way that engages a population of students that has been raised on television? How can a fair and effective accountability system for students, schools, and districts be constructed? The issues range from broad to narrow and from philosophical to technical, and all deserve attention. How they are resolved will determine the ways that principles and policies are translated into classroom realities that improve education. Two issues that go to the heart of most attempts to improve teaching and learning in the United States are our perspective on equality of opportunity and our ability to moderate our views and seek steady improvement, rather than lurch from panacea to "magic bullet."

Equality of Opportunity

A basic premise of the Clinton administration's reform proposals is that equality and excellence in the U.S. educational system are flip sides of the same coin. Without excellence, there will be no equality, because students will be denied the right to reach their potential and take advantage of opportunities. And without equitable access to quality education, there cannot be widespread excellence. Challenging standards in mathematics that expect eighth graders to use the concept of conditional probability, or in language arts that expect fourth grade students to write a short but persuasive theme, do not lead to excellence in schools unless the opportunity to meet the standards is available.

Providing full and equitable access for all, however, will take time. In the first few years of the reforms, the odds are substantial that the most needy students will be less likely than advantaged students to have the trained teachers (and other resources) that are able to provide them with the quality of curriculum and instruction that they need to achieve to the standards.

The effect, in the early years of the reforms, could be an increase in an already substantial gap between the achievement levels of the children of the poor and those of the well-to-do and between whites and African and Hispanic Americans. This gap, which closed substantially during the 1970s and through the middle 1980s, started to open wider in 1990 and 1992. While much of the recent expansion of the gap is the result of increasing poverty and other social conditions, some of it may be the product of recent reforms that are more widely available to advantaged students than to the poor and minorities.[14]

This poses a fundamental policy dilemma. Should a state or community embark on a course of reform that, over the long term, is expected to reduce disparities in opportunity and achievement among groups even if, over the short term, it arguably could increase the achievement of the more advantaged to a greater extent than that of the poor and some minorities?

On balance, I believe the answer is yes. A vigorous effort, of course, should be made to prevent a negative short-term effect; recognizing that it could happen is an added incentive at all levels to take steps to ameliorate it. But, beyond that precaution, three fundamental reasons exist for pursuing the reforms. First, a standards-based reform, focused on all students, creates a clarity of expectations that provides a powerful argument for directing the needed resources to the least advantaged students and areas. This effect will operate in the short as well as the long run.

Second, the evidence is clear that all students can learn to far more challenging standards than they have been given the opportunity up until now. Yet there are many who do not believe this and who act to make it impossible by constraining the curricular opportunities for the most needy students. Only by establishing clear standards for _all_ students can all be given a chance.

Third, I do not believe that there is a viable alternative. Simply going forward in the same fashion as we have in the past will not redress the problems of the schools of the poor and the minorities. Standards-based reforms have at least as powerful an argument to succeed in the short run as other current strategies and a far greater opportunity for the future.

As I make this argument, I want to emphasize that standards-based reforms provide only a framework, albeit a framework that may help make policies and actions more coherent and more focused on teaching and learning. But the framework does not by itself provide the will and skill necessary to change the bureaucratic structures of large cities, or to engage teachers who are "burned out," or to energize parents who are living in or on the edge of poverty, or to motivate students. The emphasis in the reforms on local flexibility and responsibility is critical—unless the reforms engage local energy and resolve, they will fail. We have the direction, knowledge, and potentially the resources to make the necessary improvements. The task, unfortunately, may be more a matter of conviction and perseverance—which makes it more difficult and more important.

The Dangers of Dogmatism

One characteristic of some education reformers and some critics is that they become zealots, simplifying their arguments to reduce ambiguity. This provides a sharp focus to their efforts, but in the long run it reduces their effectiveness because most thoughtful people know that there are no simple answers to successfully improving the quality of education. Advocates of standards-based reform are not immune to this disease. Perhaps, inadvertently, some in the reform movement are becoming associated with dogmatic ways of approaching educational change in the same manner that characterizes some critics of the movement. A number of issues tend to bring out strong and often rigid views.

One example is performance assessment versus short-answer testing. Some supporters of the reform efforts appear to completely reject short-answer (particularly multiple-choice) testing. While multiple-choice testing is inappropriate for some situations and complete reliance on these tests is a mistake, no evidence supports the notion that short-answer and multiple-choice items are inappropriate for use in all assessments. In fact, for the reforms to succeed, many assessments probably will rely at least partially on short-answer questions to provide a necessary breadth of coverage.

A second example is meaning versus skill development in early reading instruction. People have crusaded over this issue, yet the evidence is clear that neither approach is fully satisfactory and that sensible reading instruction blends the two, using one or the other or a mix according to the needs of students.

A third example is constructivist versus didactic teaching. A fourth is cooperative versus competitive strategies for teaching and motivating students. A fifth is "doing science" instead of "being taught" or reading about science or simulating "doing science." A sixth is not practicing spelling because it does not improve reading and writing. A seventh is "the basics" versus "higher-order thinking."

There are many other examples of extreme positions based on data that do not support absolute generalizations. These positions smack of the "magic bullet" programs and strategies that have dominated so very much of education practice.

If the reforms and their advocates are associated with extreme positions that are fundamentally indefensible, then no effective response can be made to criticize or hold off critics of the reforms who take similarly dogmatic, though opposing, positions. And, more important, the public will be misled and the reforms jeopardized. A reasonable balance must be created between advocating methods and being able to back up positions with as strong a body of evidence as possible. In advocating flexibility and responsibility, reform advocates must be flexible and responsible as well.

In a manner, the emphasis in the administration's reforms on local responsibility and flexibility responds to this issue, because critical pedagogical decisions are placed in the hands of teachers and local administrators, who should have more sense than to blindly accept the most recent panacea. But the same good sense that has local teachers reject a new panacea will also have them reject the reforms if the two are seen as associated.

A thoughtful and constructive balance in method and strategy that also sets a clear course for challenging standards responds to another concern in schools and local districts: a yearning for stability, for predictability. Many teachers and administrators desire reform but are frustrated by changing signals and policy directions. Some others may not want to do anything very differently, but, if they were required to change, would also desire consistent and coherent direction. This does not imply rigid rules and directions, but clear goals and support and the time to see that progress is being made. In both instances, the premium is on stability and predictability. Clear standards, a coherent system, and a balanced and responsible set of strategies respond to both groups.

FINAL THOUGHTS

The United States is not alone in its efforts to improve the quality of education. Internationally, tremendous experimentation is going on throughout Europe and Asia. In particular, federal systems such as those in New Zealand, Australia, Canada, and Germany are grappling with standards-based reforms and with the relationships among local, state, and federal levels in largely the same way that the United States is. Much can be learned from their experiences.

One lesson that many countries are learning is that just as coherence and focus are needed through all levels of the education system, so, too, coherence is needed over time. New ideas and programs need time to develop, grow, and adjust to changing circumstances if they are to show results. Public reporting and other accountability measures are important, but so is patience. Too many promising ideas of the past were abandoned too soon because of administrative and ideologically motivated political shifts, poor planning, and a misguided search for quick fixes. To make widespread and long-lasting improvements, reform must be implemented for the long term.

NOTES

1. This paper is a revised version of remarks given at the Brookings Institution seminar on "Systemic Education Reform." I want to thank Brett Scoll, Jessica Levin, Jennifer O'Day, Val Plisko, Jeff Rodamar, David Stevenson, Brenda Turnbull, and Joanne Wiggins for comments on an earlier version.

2. Testimony of Marshall S. Smith before the Subcomittee on Government Management, Information and Technology of the House Committee on Government Reform and Oversight, May 23, 1995; and National Center for Education Statistics, *The Condition of Education 1994* (U.S. Department of Education, 1994), especially pp. 2-6.

3. Organization for Economic Cooperation and Development, *OECD Economic Surveys: United States, 1993-1994* (OECD, 1994).

4. The standards-based reform strategy has been widely written about and is supported by a great variety of business, governmental and education groups. See Marshall S. Smith and Jennifer O'Day, "Systemic School Reform," in S. Fuhrman and B. Malen, eds., *The Politics of Curriculum and Testing: The 1990 Yearbook of the Politics of Education Associations* (Philadelphia: Falmer Press, 1991); and Competitiveness Policy Council, *Building a Standards-Based School System: Report of the Education SubCouncil to the Competitiveness Policy Council* (Washington, 1993).

5. "Struggling for Standards," *Education Week* Special Report, April 12, 1995.

6. In many respects the NCTM standards appear to have been successful. Since publication in 1989, they have been adopted in form or reality in a significant number of states and communities and have had a substantial influence on textbooks, teacher training, and assessments. There is even some evidence of a measurable effect on practice. National Council of Teachers of Mathematics, *Curriculum and Evaluation Standards for School Mathematics* (Reston, Va., 1989); National Council of Teachers of Mathematics, *Road to Reform, A Mathematics Education: How Far Have We Traveled?* results of a pilot study conducted for the NCTM (Reston, Va., 1992); D. Ball and others, *Understanding State Efforts to Reform Teaching and Learning: The Progress of Instructional Reform in Schools for Disadvantaged Children* (Department of Education and National Science Foundation, 1994); and A. Porter, J. Smithson, and E. Osthoff, "Standard Setting as a Strategy for Upgrading High School Mathematics and Science," in R. Elmore and S. Fuhrman, eds., *The Governance of Curriculum: The 1994 ASCD Yearbook* (Alexandria, Va.: Association for Supervision and Curriculum Development, 1994).

7. See Lee S. Shulman, "Teaching Alone, Learning Together: Needed Agendas for the New Reforms," in T. J. Sergiovanni and John H. Moore, eds., *Schooling for Tomorrow: Directing Reforms to Issues That Count* (Boston: Allyn and Bacon, 1989); Andrew Hargraves and Michael G. Fullan, *Understanding*

Teacher Development (New York: Teachers College Press, 1992); Judith W. Little, "Teacher Professional Development in a Climate of Educational Reform," *Educational Evaluation and Policy Analysis*, vol. 15, no. 2 (1993), pp. 129–51; and David K. Cohen, Milbrey W. McLaughlin, and Joan E. Talbert, eds., *Teaching for Understanding: Challenges for Policy and Practice* (San Francisco: Jossey-Bass, 1993).

8. See Smith and O'Day, "Systemic School Reform"; D. K. Cohen and J. P. Spillane, "Policy and Practice: The Relations between Governance and Instruction," in G. Grant, ed., *Review of Research in Education*, no. 18 (Washington: American Education Research Association, 1992); and Susan Fuhrman, ed., *Designing Coherent Education Policy: Improving the System* (San Francisco: Jossey-Bass, 1993).

9. See Linda Darling-Hammond, "Instructional Policy into Practice: The Power of the Bottom Over the Top," *Education Evaluation and Policy Analysis*, vol. 12, no. 3 (1990), pp. 233-42; and Karen S. Louis and Matthew Miles, *Improving the Urban High School: What Works and Why* (New York: Teachers College Press, 1990).

10. See Jennifer O'Day and Marshall Smith, "Systemic Reform and Educational Opportunity," in Fuhrman, ed., *Designing Coherent Education Policy.*

11. In brief, the goals declare that by the year 2000 all students will arrive at school ready to learn; the high school graduation rate will be at least 90 percent; students will be competent in core academic subjects; U.S. students will be first in the world in math and science; all adults will be literate and skilled; every school will be free of drugs and violence; teachers will have greater opportunities for professional development; and every school will promote partnerships to increase parental involvement in education. For a short paper that provides some interesting assessments of the chances for the nation's accomplishing the third and fourth goals, see Cathy Casserly and Martin Carnoy, "The National Education Goals 2000, Changing Demographics of the Under 18 Population and U.S. Achievement Trends: Are They Compatible?" (New Brunswick, N.J.: Consortium for Policy Research in Education, 1994). This is not the place to defend or analyze the goals. Though undoubtedly overly ambitious, they will continue to help serve the basic purpose of helping to keep the nation's attention focused on the challenge of improving its schools.

12. National Council on Education Standards and Testing, *Raising Standards for American Education* (Washington, 1992), especially appendix F.

13. It is worth noting that NESIC has no legislative or other necessary relationship to the National Assessment of Educational Progress (NEAP).

14. See Marshall Smith and Jennifer O'Day, "Educational Equality: 1966 and Now," in D. A. Verstegen and J. G. Ward, eds., *Spheres of Justice in Education: The 1990 American Education Finance Association Yearbook* (New York:

Harper Business, 1991); O'Day and Smith, "Systemic Reform and Educational Opportunity"; and U.S. Department of Education, *NAEP 1992 Trends in Academic Progress* (1994), especially the data on the expanding gap between very disadvantaged and advantaged urban residents.

THEODORE R. SIZER

Will National Standards and Assessments Make a Difference?

Will national standards and assessments make a difference?

They certainly will, and they already have; most of it, so far, is good. The focus on standards is pushing into public discussion a definition of what kids should be able to do with their minds and, in so doing, has raised some issues that have always been below the surface and should not be.

First, what is meant by *standards*? Mastery of skills and knowledge? Or understanding, in the sense that Howard Gardner and David Perkins describe? Or perhaps habits? That is, are the highest standards exemplified by what kids do when they are not being observed? Are the highest standards the way kids appear, instinctively, to use their minds and knowledge as a result of their formal schooling?

Second, what guarantees exist that the kids will meet the standards, however defined? This question of assessment has provoked wonderfully rich debate and some very important new research. Most persistent has been the challenge of standardized testing, both on technical grounds and on grounds that the qualities of mind it often displays are not considered worthwhile.

The consideration of assessment raises matters circling around the commonly used word *authenticity*. That is, measure what kids can really do, not tokens of what kids can do—assess their real work. Furthermore, the question of assessment ties back to the definition of the standards. If habits of mind—what kids do when nobody is looking—are important, evolve a different kind of assessment than if a measure is sought of the immediate mastery of skills and knowledge.

Again, the debate is wonderfully rich and exceedingly useful, and exceedingly upsetting because the debate is exposing issues long hidden. To focus on national goals sounds good. The nation is going to gird up its collective loins. Such a commitment puffs up an America that is in a period of extraordinary uncertainty. The notion of "taking charge nationally" is one that massages the current emotional distress.

Fostering common national standards is acceptable at the margins. (Can the child read or not? Can the adolescent understand an insurance form or not?) It gets tough beyond the obvious. National standards for American history? National standards for literature? National standards for biological sciences? Maybe there is no common ground. Maybe there should not be.

The process of establishing the standards repeatedly raises the question of who sets them. When you or I or some commission demands that "we" must have standards, who is "we"? And what right do "we," as defined, have to do those things? We—whoever we are—are dealing with youngsters' minds and hearts, a matter of their fundamental intellectual freedom. No freedom is more precious in a democracy than intellectual freedom. The question of who the "we" is is not a trivial one; it is a fundamental one. In the current debate, the issue has been avoided.

Americans are fearful. There is a sense abroad of a country unhinged. Deep skepticism exists about America's ability to govern itself, and an almost savage scapegoating takes place of any person who puts his or her profile high enough to address the American condition. If one stands back from the words and senses the language in the political air, one finds it apocalyptic, often self-righteous. It has been so for twenty to twenty-five years but has become more noticeable since the early 1980s.

Disciplined civic discourse, to use Amy Gutmann's phrase, is feared. Letting the profound disagreements come up and be addressed in an uncontrolled—not in a controlled (meaning smothered or dismissed)—setting is anxiety producing. Disorder is alarming. One recalls Robert Wiebe's *The Search for Order*. Early Progressive reforms reflect a belief in systems.

The word *system* has come up again; endless talk is heard about systemic reform. Essentially, it implies a technocratic approach. Reflect on the nice Progressive superintendent. Superintendents of systems now exist. The word is revealing. Underneath is a distrust of democracy, particularly of local democracy. The belief is that the locals will prove incompetent. Proposals are made to give "school sites" and "parent councils" some running room, but "we" (whoever we are) always reserve the right to snatch it back.

While historical analogies are always frightfully imperfect, rereading the *Report of the Committee of Ten,* issued in 1893, is instructive, particularly when laid against the 1983 *A Nation at Risk* and *The New Basics* and all of that ilk. Read again J. M. Rice's early 1890s pieces on schooling and poverty and then read Jonathan Kozol. The parallels are stunning.

The Progressive response was for a system driven by "silence" and run by "experts" who were to the greatest extent possible insulated from politics. Did it work? Should it be reinvented?

An astonishingly quick shift has taken place over recent years in American political expectations toward a federal or national role for the substance of schooling. As Ernest Boyer said, what has emerged would have been unthinkable when he was U.S. commissioner of education in the 1970s. Dwight D. Eisenhower must be rolling over in his grave. Franklin D. Roosevelt would laugh, and Harry Hopkins would lose his temper.

Why has a national or federal role been so quickly accepted in the setting of standards that are voluntary yet aligned with all the checks and balances that Marshall S. Smith described in the Clinton administration's proposal? Why is this centralization being accepted without searching discussion? Why has that discussion not been insisted upon? The question then arises of who are we to take charge? Who is the "we"?

The disinterest of the press boggles the mind. Coverage of the signing in San Diego of Goals 2000 was relegated to page 36 in the lower left-hand corner. To the Northeastern newspapers, such as the *New York Times,* the reception on May 16, 1994, in the Rose Garden was a nonevent. Why is the public media so inattentive to a tidal shift in the American political system's sense of responsibility for the quality of education?

The only group that is attentive is the radical right. In 1990 I was invited by Colorado governor Roy Romer to his house. To gain entry, I had to cross a picket line. Placards saying "go home" were carried by school-age kids—during the school day. Fear appears to be driving the movement—fear of losing control, fear of some distant figure or figures deciding outcomes.

Four critical points must be considered in any discussion of standards and assessments. First, standards and assessments designed by people remote from the immediacy of schools will likely not be rigorous. The current system of "standards from a distance" is likely to produce relatively unteachable, mediocre, run-of-the-mill stuff and is

created by people who are not accountable, either to a relevant electorate or to the demanding discipline of having to teach toward those
standards. If anybody who is involved in setting the standards in
mathematics should be required to have to teach it publicly for three
years, the response would be different. Schools are "street-level" enter-
prises, to use Michael Lipsky's useful and accurate formulation.
Ultimately, what happens of consequence happens at the lowest level,
willy-nilly.

The 1950s produced a seemingly endless stream of reports from
commissions, committees, and associations about learning. Almost
without exception, most of the recommendations involved too much
coverage, particularly at the high school level. School curricula are a
mile wide and an inch deep. For example, what could be absolutely
more insane than the world history course, Cleopatra to Clinton in 180
days? What could be absolutely more insane than an English teacher
with 130 kids, five classes a day, expected to edit childish writing into
prose of quality and grace and clarity?

Second, there is log rolling. "We" want lots of things done in our
schools, and "we" traditionally appoint committees that engage in "I'll
get my priority and you'll get yours." Even the Committee of Ten (in
spite of the fearsome chairmanship of Charles W. Eliot) was guilty of
it; more recent committees report to more subject areas than were identified by the Committee of Ten.

Note the log rolling of the core subjects and goals since 1983. They
have changed and lengthened three times, each in response to the
pressure of particular special interest groups. Politics has led to the
dropping of one subject and the adding of another, only to be changed
again. The six national goals are now, what, seven in number? Or is it
eight? Maybe by tomorrow it will be nine. The process is, essentially,
political, and much of it has nothing to do with children and teaching.
There is no rationale for log rolling.

Third, most current recommendations reinforce the factory
metaphor; they are lists. "These are the things that will be covered.
These are the things that I, the teacher, will put into the head of the student." All of this is preceded by lofty rhetoric about the quality of
thinking and so forth and so on—but the lists follow. Many committee
reports embody a complete disjunction between the stated goals and
the actual recommendations. Little incentive exists in the process to
pay careful attention to the growing understandings from cognitive

science, particularly in the rich differences among children in the ways of learning and thinking.

Fourth, little more than rhetorical concern is displayed for the "savage inequalities" of America's "two nations" of schools, for the kind of horror that is mentioned in the metropolitan sections of every city newspaper. I was at a high school in Chicago last winter. Six kids had been killed by handguns since September. One murder took place right in front of the school. Folks at the street level understand about the horror. Educators must confront the reality that 20 to 35 percent of American kids are growing up in terror.

Thoughtful Americans are puzzled by the paucity of careful analysis of why American schools are so mindless and weak. Among the many possible causes, only one is the lack of national goals, standards, and assessments. The goal statements of tens of dozens of high schools across the United States read almost the same. They are variations on the theme of the 1918 *Cardinal Principles of Education Report,* and they deal with intellectual, health, civic duty, and other matters. What is so astonishingly common is a set of rhetorical standards, which are studiously ignored even if put up on the school walls every ten years when the accreditors come around.

American secondary schools, in particular, all operate in relatively the same way. They are driven by the same beliefs and traditions. They differ primarily in terms of social class; there is gruel for poor kids and richer fare for well-to-do kids.

Overwhelming evidence is available that the way schools are set up—the ideas upon which they are based—are well intentioned but profoundly flawed. The ideas go back to 1900. It is time to challenge them, to rip their insides out and to rebuild them.

The heart of the matter is the way schools operate and the ideas underlying the current design. They are not "learning communities." They are not places that are respectful of individuals, including the teachers. They also do not address the chaos of growing up in America today, not only in the inner city and in the poor rural areas, but also in the suburbs. Differences in growing up must be faced in a fundamental and not just rhetorical way.

Further, thoughtful teachers will say that you cannot separate ends from means. You cannot say, "Well, somebody up there will give you the ends (what students should know and be able to do), and you do the means." As a teacher with thirty years of experience, I know that cannot work. Unless I have some authority over the ends, I cannot devise the means.

There is plenty of rhetoric abroad about the weaknesses of the hierarchical bureaucracy, but—ironically, perhaps—the status quo is persistently reinforced in most policy discussions. The savagery of the attack on hierarchical bureaucracy in the work of John Chubb and Terry Moe has been largely ignored. By and large, the hierarchical bureaucracy still is expected to be in the permission-giving business, now more than ever.

Teachers are skeptical of the notion that school alone is the locus of all education. Again, the reports of earlier decades are instructive. *Youth: Transition to Adulthood,* which Jim Coleman and others published during the first Nixon administration, makes a distinction between an information-poor and an information-rich culture. The early 1990s are information-rich, far beyond what Coleman and his colleagues were seeing in the early 1970s. The most powerful public education system the United States has ever had is called the mass media. Yet the discussion over the public's right of access to the mass media is not addressed. The mass media have to do with commercial interests—there is nothing wrong with that—but no public claim is made on the media for public education purposes. The discussion of education reform goes on as though the media did not exert such a powerful force on America's children.

So much for the criticism. What makes sense? First, powerful examples must be made available of rigorous student work, all kinds of examples. Push the real work out there. Take videos of students hard at it. Teachers should not be given only lists; give them lots of images of good work. And honor the differences represented. Recall, for example, the 1960s and the reform of high school physics. The Feds financed two major projects, Jerrold Zacharias's PSSC and Gerald Holton's Project Physics. Both were good science; each had a coherent approach. Zacharias and Holton would not sit together in the same room, although they were both based in Cambridge. That was valuable because the policy was right: Rigor—but not one rigor.

Second, push on a mass basis three standards: resourceful reading, clear writing and speaking, and computational mathematics. These are subjects upon which most can agree and without which no school can begin to be effective. The point is not competence testing, but serious testing and assessment. And deliberately keep central authority out of the other elements of school, matters over which there can and should be "no one best standard."

Schools should be required to issue annual reports. Annual public exhibitions should be held. Schools must have the autonomy to move their work forward, but the state, through inspection, should oversee and guide, not dictate. The power should remain where the parent can look into the eye of the person who has the power to change the decision about a matter of fundamental importance in the intellectual education of the child. Simply, the "we" should be parent-child-community.

ANDREW C. PORTER

The Uses and Misuses of Opportunity-to-Learn Standards

In 1994 standards-based education reform in the United States appeared to get a major boost with the passage of the Goals 2000: Educate America Act. Less than one year later, however, much of what that legislation called for was being rethought by the 104th Congress. One of the most contested pieces of Goals 2000 was opportunity-to-learn (OTL) standards, which the legislation defined as "the criteria for, and the basis of, assessing the sufficiency or quality of the resources, practices, and conditions necessary to each level of the education system (schools, local educational agencies, and states) to provide all students with an opportunity to learn the material in voluntary national content standards or state content standards."[1] Behind this rather sterile and innocuous definition of OTL standards, however, lies a sea of controversy concerning such issues as local control, school accountability, and student certification.

To proponents, OTL standards represent the solution to age-old problems of equity in education. In particular, advocates of OTL standards see them as an appropriate antidote to the potentially negative effects of high-stakes testing on students who, through no fault of their own, attend schools that provide an inferior education. For opponents, OTL standards evoke all their worst fears about federal intrusion into local control of the quality and nature of education. By 1995 it appeared that the voluntary national OTL standards as called for in Goals 2000 would never come to be. At the state level, however, OTL standards were still under consideration, and in several cases states were moving ahead with conceptualization and implementation of OTL standards. Professional organizations also could get increasingly involved in the development of OTL standards.

Do OTL standards have the potential for helping to solve the problem of providing equality of educational opportunity to all students, or are OTL standards simply a strategy for derailing recent efforts to move educational accountability away from its old focus on inputs and processes and toward a new focus on accountability in terms of educational outcomes? Are OTL standards simply one more strategy by professional educators to get more federal, state, and local money pumped into the K-12 education system? Will OTL standards represent another step, along with such ideas as a state curricula and state student achievement test, in what appears to be a slow and steady march away from local control of education? Are OTL standards yet one more education issue that divides Democrats from Republicans?

The answers to these questions are not yet available; OTL standards are at the emerging idea stage. Neither the what nor the why of OTL standards has yet been finalized.

ORIGINS OF OTL STANDARDS

The initial motivation for OTL standards stems from an equity concern that high-stakes assessments of student achievement are fair only if students have had an adequate opportunity to learn the content assessed in those high-stakes tests. This concern is not a new issue for education. In 1981 the courts ruled that Florida could not use a test as a standard for determining high school graduation unless Florida first established that all students had an opportunity to learn the material tested.[2] Nearly a decade later, however, concerns about the fairness of high-stakes testing had escalated substantially. Both the National Council on Education Standards and Testing (NCEST) and the New Standards Project, led by Lauren B. Resnick and Marc Tucker, called for assessments of student achievement against new and demanding educational standards.[3] In both cases, considerable enthusiasm was evident for making student performance on the new and demanding assessments have consequences both immediately in school and for future evaluations by colleges and employers. Establishing opportunity to learn for a minimum competency test such as that used for high school graduation in Florida is much easier than establishing opportunity to learn for assessments designed against the ambitious curriculum reforms of the late 1980s, such as those reflected in the National Council of Teachers of Mathematics' *Curriculum and Evaluation Standards for School Mathematics* and the American Association for the

Advancement of Science's *Science for All Americans*.[4] Both NCEST and the New Standards Project suggested something along the lines of OTL standards as a solution to the fairness problem. In the case of the New Standards Project, a social compact was constructed to ensure that states, districts, and schools would not use performance on new assessments to determine credentials until all students being assessed had an opportunity to prepare themselves. In the case of NCEST, school delivery standards were recommended to ensure that each student in a school has a fair opportunity to achieve the knowledge and skills in the national content standards, with the assumption that assessments would be aligned to the content standards.

While fairness in high-stakes assessment was a problem easily understood by most, the solutions to that problem, New Standards' social compact and NCEST's school delivery standards, lacked definition. In essence, they were nothing more than place holders for solutions. In response, the National Governors' Association (NGA) undertook the task of developing and analyzing what school delivery standards might be. The result is a series of four commissioned papers, testimony from an NGA–sponsored hearing on OTL standards, and reports from four states, each given a modest $5,000 grant from NGA to think through issues involved in developing and implementing a system of OTL standards. The products of NGA work are available in *The Debate on Opportunity-to-Learn Standards*.[5]

During the first year of discussion of NCEST's recommended school delivery standards, the issue became so hotly contested that the name was changed to OTL standards. Despite the controversy and change of name, the idea remained and was next found in the final language of Goals 2000: Educate America Act.

Goals 2000 took a fairly soft stand on OTL standards, specifying that national OTL standards would be voluntary, not required, and that while states were to develop OTL standards, those standards need not be approved or even reviewed at the federal level. Further, only one use of state OTL standards was prescribed: When a school has been identified as weak, that school must develop a plan for improvement, and that plan must draw on OTL standards. The act did authorize the secretary of education to award grants on a competitive basis to consortia of individuals and organizations to develop voluntary national OTL standards and to develop a listing of model programs for use on a voluntary basis by states. The language of the act made absolutely clear the desire to avoid any appearance of federal requirements for OTL standards: "No State shall be required to obtain certification of standards or assessments developed . . . or to participate in programs under title III of this Act, as a condition of participating in any federal education program under this or any other Act."[6]

Despite the softness in the approach of Goals 2000 toward OTL standards, concerns over the possibility of inappropriate federal intrusions into state and local education practices did not go away. Heated debate between Democrats and Republicans and between the House and the Senate about the appropriate role for national OTL standards that took place during the development and passage of Goals 2000 erupted again one year later when Republicans took control of both the House and the Senate. From the very beginning, Republicans had wanted OTL standards to be dropped completely from the legislation, while Democrats wanted OTL standards to be required of all states.

Predicting what will happen to OTL standards is impossible. At the federal level, OTL standards might yet become as prominent as the soft language in Goals 2000 suggests. More likely, Goals 2000 language on OTL standards will be diluted; quite possibly OTL standards could disappear from federal legislation altogether. Nevertheless, the issue of opportunity to learn will not disappear from American education. After all, as R. F. Elmore and S. H. Fuhrman concluded: "States already have an accumulation of input regulations that have as their essential purpose the assurance of equal access to learning."[7] Most states have minimum standards for student attendance and teacher qualifications. Most states have minimum per student funding standards. States have curriculum frameworks, minimum course requirements for high school graduation, guidelines for time to be spent on each subject at the elementary school level, and continuing professional development requirements for teachers and administrators. Several states have restrictions on what textbooks can be used, and some states have school accreditation programs involving site visits to schools.

Given America's history of efforts to ensure the quality of education through control of inputs and processes, the question is not whether OTL standards will disappear from state legislation, but whether states will change the ways in which they attempt to ensure that students in their jurisdiction have an adequate opportunity to learn the important academic content to which they are entitled. Concerns for fairness and equity will not go away and will be exacerbated in situations where high-stakes assessments are used for purposes of student certification and accountability. Whether or not the term *OTL standards* continues to be used or not, the issues that motivated OTL standards at the time of Goals 2000 passage will continue. As a result and despite signs that the U.S. Congress was likely to back away from OTL standards at the federal level, the Council of Chief State School Officers adopted opportunity-to-learn standards as a priority area for work by that organization in 1995. At the same time, several states around the nation continue their work on OTL standards as one important part of their overall strategies to support school improvement and to guarantee adequate educational experiences for all students.

USING OPPORTUNITY-TO-LEARN STANDARDS

OTL standards are intended to become a useful mechanism for ensuring access to a high-quality education for all students, regardless of their gender, race, family economic level, or geographic location. This is what is called for in the national education goals, and this is the hallmark of the curriculum reforms of the late 1980s. All students in the United States are to have access to ambitious content in the core academic subject areas, emphasizing deep conceptual understanding, the ability to use one's knowledge to reason and to solve problems, and the ability to communicate effectively. But exactly what are OTL standards, and how are they to be used? These two basic questions are interrelated, with answers to one depending on answers to the other.

OTL Standards and School Accountability

When school delivery standards were introduced by NCEST (and the social compact introduced by the New Standards Project), the idea was to make high-stakes accountability for students based on their achievement conditioned on schools' providing students an adequate opportunity to learn. This use of OTL standards had legal precedent in the *Debra P.* v. *Turlington* case concerning the administration of a minimum competency test to certify high school graduation in Florida. Students were to be held accountable according to their measured achievement, but only if they attended a school judged to have provided them with an adequate opportunity to learn. Schools, on the other hand, were to be held accountable for having the inputs and procedures required in the school delivery standards (OTL standards). As has been pointed out elsewhere, such an approach runs head on into a number of difficulties that seem virtually certain to stand in the way of protecting students from a bad education.[8]

For OTL standards to improve the quality of education, schools would need to be motivated to meet the OTL standards. Motivation might be high for schools attempting to protect their academic reputation (or even schools wishing to build an academic reputation), but these schools are most likely to meet the OTL standards anyway. The schools that fail to provide an adequate education are already fairly well known, at least in a general way, and yet progress toward improving the quality of their education has not occurred. If motivation is the problem, failing to meet OTL standards would not help.

Even if all schools were motivated to provide an adequate education to all students, some schools lack the resources to do so. Resources broadly include teacher knowledge and skill as well as what money can buy: a decent physical plant, up-to-date instructional materials, computing and communication technology. Were OTL standards to be used for school accountability, some schools likely would meet the standards immediately, while other schools less motivated or having fewer resources might never meet the standards. This creates a dilemma for student accountability. Either student accountability would have to wait until all schools had been certified as meeting the OTL standards, or student accountability would need to be phased in school by school. Neither alternative seems acceptable. If student accountability must wait on all schools meeting OTL standards, either those standards would be set low enough to be meaningless or student accountability would be put off indefinitely. If standards were to be phased in school by school, then some students would do well on the high-stakes assessments, other students would do poorly, and other students would not even get a score because their school was found to provide an inadequate education. This scenario clearly suggests that a student who has received an inadequate education cannot be protected. The real issue is not how to protect a student who has been disadvantaged by an inferior education from the sanctions of a high-stakes assessment. That would be treating the symptom, not the cause. The real issue is how to provide all students with an adequate education, regardless of whether they will be subsequently tested for whatever purposes.

For those who believe in the need for school and student account-ability, what approach, then, makes sense? A focus on the fairness of high-stakes assessment is misleading. What is fundamentally unfair is to deny certain students access to an adequate education because of their gender, race, family income, or geographic setting. School and student accountability must lead to a situation in which, on the one hand, all students do their best with whatever opportunities their schools supply and, on the other hand, all schools do their best to pro-vide high-quality educational experiences for all students. Because the goal is student learning, the focus for both types of accountability should be on what students can accomplish in the core academic con-tent areas. This approach puts a premium on having reliable assess-ments of student achievement that are carefully aligned to ambitious content standards.

States wishing to implement school and student accountability based on assessments of student achievement should allow a period of time in which the assessments are given and the results disseminated without consequences. This would allow the schools and the students to get used to what is being assessed and would allow both to take whatever corrective actions seem appropriate. One hopes that instruc-tion would adapt in ways necessary to provide all students the oppor-tunity to learn what is necessary to perform on the assessments.

In focusing accountability on student achievement, a host of concep-tual and technical problems must be solved. Detailing those is not the purpose here. Nevertheless, some basic ideas about outcome-oriented accountability for students and schools must be considered.

First, holding schools accountable in terms of student achievement is a much more difficult problem than holding students accountable based on their achievement. As has been argued elsewhere, a "value-added" approach makes the most sense; essentially, the idea is to determine each school's contribution to increases in its students' achievement.[9] In other words, for some period of time, say eighth grade or the middle school years, how much growth in student achievement can be attributed to having gone to a particular school? Because the focus is on schools serving all students well, these esti-mates of value added to student achievement would need to be disag-gregated according to characteristics of students (for example, gender, race, family income) to ensure rough comparability regardless of type of student served. One criticism of the value-added approach to school accountability is that schools serving students with very low achievement might show a large value added, yet still leave their students well below any acceptable level of accomplishment. Thus school accountability should take into account both an indication of the school's value added to student achievement as well as an indication of the overall level of performance at the end of the period of time under investigation. Schools meeting the standard would have both high student post-test scores as well as high value added. Schools clearly failing the standard would have both low value added and low scores. Schools in between would either have high value added and low scores or high scores and low value added.

Second, both schools and students should be held accountable on the same measures of student accomplishment. Examples currently exist of schools being held accountable for student performance on measures of student performance that have no consequences for the students. In Kentucky, this may have resulted in seniors in high school not taking the state assessment seriously, even though the consequences for their schools were serious. Similarly, some high-stakes tests for students, such as one used to determine high school graduation, have no direct consequences for schools based on those same assessments. Achievement is the product of what students and schools do together. Thus an accountability system should simultaneously hold schools and students accountable on the same achievement measures.

Third, school accountability in terms of student achievement keeps the focus on the ultimate goal, while leaving schools free to pursue the goal according to their own local demands and opportunities. A focus on inputs and processes would end up controlling factors that are only loosely coupled to student achievement. Past approaches to accountability in education that hold students accountable for their tested achievement, but hold their schools accountable for inputs and processes, are out of balance. This is especially true given that no known functional relationship exists between the inputs and processes of schooling, on the one hand, and student achievement, on the other. In short, detailed prescriptions of what schools should do to ensure high student achievement are not yet available (and many would argue will never be).

Accountability enthusiasts may endorse both accountability in terms of student achievement and accountability in terms of school inputs and procedures. Alternatively, accountability in terms of both procedures and outputs might happen by default, because school bureaucracies are notorious for keeping old rules and procedures on the books while taking on new rules and procedures that might be at cross purposes. In either case, school accountability simultaneously on both student achievement and school processes would place schools in a double bind that should be avoided. Either inputs and processes should be set and outcomes assumed, or outcomes should be specified and flexibility granted to pursue those outcomes. Holding schools accountable on outcomes, leaving schools discretion on matters of how to pursue those outcomes, recognizes that education requires professional judgment and that providing an adequate education is not a simple matter that can be ensured a priori by following a formula-like checklist of dos and don'ts about resources and procedures.[10]

Some say that accountability on student outcomes is not feasible because of serious technical problems. They worry that current tests tap only a narrow slice of the desired curriculum, placing an inappropriately heavy emphasis upon students' abilities to memorize facts and master routine skills.[11] They worry that performance assessment, still in its early stages of development, will not have the technical properties necessary for individual student certification (which places a premium on accuracy), nor the broad validity that school accountability would require (if it is to serve as a mechanism for prodding schools into curriculum upgrading). Initial efforts at performance assessment have largely fallen short of the high standards that student and school accountability require. On-demand performance assessments involve tasks that take substantial amounts of time, making the number of tasks sampled relatively small. Low task-to-task correlations have yielded low task sampling reliability, especially at the individual student level.[12] But experimentation with performance assessments for purposes of external accountability is relatively new, and progress is being made. Besides, for purposes of accountability, student achievement might be measured in a variety of ways, including on-demand performance assessment, portfolio assessment, and even some old-fashioned multiple-choice and short-answer assessment. In the aggregate, these multiple forms of assessment might provide valid and reliable information at both the student and the school level while at the same time serving as an appropriate mechanism for driving instruction by providing an accurate reflection of what is wanted.

The technical challenges in developing assessments of student achievement are no more daunting than the technical challenges of assessing opportunity to learn. While a detailed analysis of the technical problems of measuring OTL must await further development of the concept, a sense of the challenges can be seen by reviewing the scope an OTL measure would require. If the goal is to certify that a school has provided all students with an adequate education, then OTL would need to be measured for each academic subject assessed; described for every different type of student the school served; be based on all courses, all sections, and all teachers; and reflect what happens most of the time (as opposed to one or two days when an observer is present). The information on OTL would need to be objective and replicable. In that sense, self-reporting from teachers and schools would not be satisfactory for accountability purposes. Just as student achievement is a function of the types of students served as well as the quality of education provided, so, too, quality instruction may be easier to provide to healthy, highly motivated students with excellent entry skills. Thus some type of adjustment for student body composition might be necessary when using OTL for purposes of school accountability, just as adjustments for prior student achievement are necessary when using student achievement for purposes of school accountability. The technical challenges to measuring OTL for purposes of school accountability would be formidable.

Thus far, discussion of school accountability has kept OTL standards distinct from student achievement. They may not always be as distinct as this analysis has made them sound. Increasingly, the architects of portfolio assessment are asking hard questions about the design and structure of a student's portfolio. In the earliest thinking, a portfolio was simply a sample of a student's work or, perhaps more narrowly, a sample of a student's best work. But as the architects of portfolio assessment made progress in defining and using scoring rubrics, they discovered that for too many portfolios no overlap existed between what the rubric was demanding and what the samples of student work offered. For example, if a student's portfolio is comprised of a collection of a student's best efforts on drill-and-practice in mathematics computation, then the student's portfolio cannot be scored on ability to solve novel problems. With no information about problem solving ability in the portfolio, the student's score must remain undefined. To solve this problem, increasingly architects of portfolio assessment are experimenting with requirements about the types of work that must be represented in a portfolio. If content standards are used to design specifications for the types of work that every portfolio must contain, then portfolios become a mechanism for defining OTL standards as well as an instrument for assessing student achievement.

The more structure required of a portfolio, the more intrusive the portfolio becomes. Teachers may choose not to follow the OTL requirements, although, if portfolios are used in student and school accountability, the pressure to meet portfolio requirements may be more than teachers can resist. Structured portfolios would make OTL standards and student achievement complementary parts of school accountability. For a school to do well, the school would need to provide students the required opportunities to learn and the students would need to learn from those opportunities in ways that were captured by the portfolios. The approach seems promising as a part of a school accountability program, though the idea requires further development and experimentation.

OTL Standards and School Improvement

OTL standards may have some value for schools that are already motivated to improve. According to David Green, Her Majesty's inspector of schools in England and senior consultant to school quality review in New York State, "The potential of engaging the teachers in a school, district or state in the everyday inspection of their own work is enormous. Certainly if focused on teaching and learning, it could provide the foundations for real and ongoing improvement in what students come to know and be able to do."[13] Using OTL standards to support school improvement is analogous to using content standards, such as the National Council of Teachers of Mathematics (NCTM) math standards, to support school improvement. The intention is to provide a convincing message of how schools need to change if the national education goals are to be reached. There are two ways in which OTL standards might assist school improvement.

The first is to provide a vision of good practice. The curriculum reforms of the late 1980s demand that schools and teachers provide a type of instruction that has been rare. Further, this excellent instruction is to be available to students from low-income families as well as to students from affluent families. Most schools and teachers would like to provide high-quality instruction, but few, if any, have relevant experience on which they can draw. They desperately need guideposts to point the ways in which their practice needs to change. OTL standards grounded in research on effective instructional practices and school strategies might provide these much-needed guideposts. An example is NCTM's *Professional Standards for Teaching Mathematics.*[14] This less well-known relative of the NCTM *Curriculum and Evaluation Standards for School Mathematics* is a 196-page document providing standards for teaching mathematics, the evaluation of the teaching of mathematics, the professional development of teachers of mathematics, and the support and development of mathematics teachers and teaching. The section most relevant to providing a vision of what good teaching of NCTM–like mathematics would entail is the approximately forty-page section on teaching of mathematics. The document stops far short of a plan of action that teachers can follow. Still it does illustrate with examples and narrative the types of activities teachers might use to promote student mastery of the NCTM content standards. OTL standards might also communicate a vision of good instruction through instructional programs, such as Cognitively Guided Instruction and Success for All.[15] These programs are based on research and have been carefully tested to establish their effectiveness in promoting student learning. Regardless of the medium, OTL standards should not be static. They must be continually updated with new research and development work to communicate the properties of effective instruction for ambitious content standards.

Without a vision, most educators will lack direction about how their practice needs to change. But a vision must do more than simply clarify what is desired. It must also inspire educators to want to improve their practice. Building a vision that meets these challenges will not be easy. But in addition to being clear and inspiring, any vision must meet a third requirement; it must be supported by empirical validation. Educational programs have come and gone over the years. The considerable popularity of today's new education programs attests to their clarity of desired practice and inspirational properties. Too many of these programs, however, represent no more than educated guesses about what will result in improved student learning of worthwhile content. Too often empirical evidence of effectiveness has not been gathered before widescale promotion of programs has occurred. OTL visions must not repeat these mistakes.

OTL standards also might support school improvement through development of a system of school process indicators.[16] First, indicators of OTL can provide valuable descriptive information about the nature of schooling. What types of schools provide what types of education to what types of students? Do students from poor families have the same opportunity to learn higher-order thinking and problem solving as do students from affluent families? Are instructional resources as available to students in one geographic location as they are to students in another? OTL standards can provide basic descriptive information about the quantity and quality of instruction being provided by schools. Second, OTL indicators can serve as a mechanism for monitoring progress in education reform. To what extent is the enacted school curriculum in alignment with the professional content standards? Is the degree of alignment improving over time? Third, a system of OTL indicators can help to diagnose causes of unsatisfactory performance of the education system. When levels of student achievement are found to be low, questions remain about why. OTL indicators can offer hypotheses by showing the relationship between various aspects of students' opportunity to learn and student achievement.

OTL indicator data could be collected on a probability sample of schools and would not need to be collected every year, because the purposes are largely descriptive rather than school-by-school accountability. Typically, indicator data are not collected longitudinally, which makes them relatively inexpensive, on the one hand, but not terribly useful for establishing causal relationships, on the other. Currently, indicator data about the nature of instruction offered to students are extremely limited. Data exist on the types of courses students take, but virtually no information about the nature of instruction within those courses. Some information is available about the preparation of teachers, but virtually none about the ways that teachers actually teach.

Using OTL standards to provide a vision of good instruction or to create a system of school process indicators differs from using OTL standards for school accountability in important ways. First, OTL accountability would force schools to do what they might not otherwise have done. In contrast, the NCTM professional standards and other similar vision-type OTL standards offer assistance as schools seek to increase student outputs. Similarly, indicator data do not tell schools what they must do but provide information to schools that may assist them in identifying where changes are needed. Second, OTL accountability would be prescriptive, requiring particular school inputs and practices. There is nothing prescriptive about a vision, which is general and suggestive, or about indicators, which provide information but stop short of specifying how that information must be used.

If OTL standards were developed to provide inspiring visions of good teaching and schooling, and if a system of OTL indicators were put in place to monitor progress that educators make as they pursue those visions, a great deal of good might be done. However, neither the vision nor the indicators would ensure that the quality of education improved. In addition, improvement would require that teachers and administrators accept greater responsibility for the achievement of their students and that the system provide the support that committed schools and teachers need to modify their practices so that all students reach the new and ambitious content standards. These changes would require fundamental shifts in incentive structures and a total rethinking of approaches to staff development. But for those educators who are already committed and who have access to resources needed for improvement, OTL standards in the form of visions of good instruction and OTL indicators to monitor progress could be quite helpful.

What Should OTL Standards Include?

Most of what has been said and written about OTL standards has been general and without reference to a particular use. Goals 2000 legislation specified that voluntary national OTL standards include availability to students of good curricula, instructional materials, and technologies; teachers capable of providing high-quality instruction; educators with access to professional development; safe and secure school facilities; and school policies that ensure nondiscrimination. In addition, curriculum, instructional practices, and assessments were to be consistent with voluntary national content standards. These requirements were to apply to OTL standards regardless of how they might be used.

Some suggest that OTL standards should address funding for education. But funding is only loosely coupled to the quality of education students receive and even more loosely to what students learn. Research has questioned whether a positive relationship exists between funding of education and student achievement, although subsequent reanalyses of these data conclude that money does matter.[17] Money is a necessary but not sufficient condition for providing quality education. For these reasons, school finance is shifting its focus away from equality in funding and toward adequacy of funding to produce desired student achievement.[18]

Schools cannot be held accountable for how much money they receive; state and federal programs and local taxpayer support determine school funding levels. Neither can schools be held accountable for providing services beyond their financial means. A fear some educators have of OTL standards is that they will be used by states, and possibly even the federal government, to require a quality and quantity of education services well beyond what current spending can afford. Regardless of the use to be made of OTL standards, funding should probably not be a part of the OTL standards' definition.

Some suggest that OTL standards should include school governance. For example, OTL standards might address the extent to which a school has control over hiring and firing of personnel or budget expenditures. Despite school governance being a central target for school restructuring efforts, school governance has not been shown to be an important predictor of student achievement. OTL standards should probably not include matters of school governance in their definition.

What should be included in OTL standards starts with desired end results and works systematically back from there through the problems of what teachers and schools need to do to the questions of what resources they might require. This is analogous to starting with OTL standards to provide a vision of good education and then proceeding from there to the more concrete level of indicators to track whether progress is being made. OTL standards should never be used for formal school accountability.

First and foremost, schools must provide a safe and orderly environment for students and educators. Schooling is compulsory in the United States. Students have no choice but to go to school, and most students have no choice but to go to a public school. Compulsory schooling cannot be allowed to place students in danger of violence or where their health is at risk, yet these basic standards of decency are not met in far too many U.S. schools.[19] Failure to meet basic standards has a negative impact on the attitudes that students bring to school and the quality of education they receive. But important as these concerns are, they are outweighed by what should be every student's right to a decent school environment.

Given quality-of-life basics, my focus for OTL standards would be on the direct antecedents of learning, the nature of instruction as it is experienced by students. Here I have in mind both standards concerning what is taught in schools as well as the quality of pedagogy used to engage students in that content. I would also include a concern for instructionally embedded resources. How are science labs used in the delivery of instruction? How does the library contribute to each student's educational experiences? What role does technology play in the delivery of a quality education? I am much less interested in knowing whether or not a school has a good library than in knowing how the library is used. Knowing that computers are in adequate supply in a school is misleading if, in practice, those computers are only accessed by a subset of the students or if those computers are only used for low-level remedial courses that might better have been eliminated from the curriculum in the first place.

For states or others developing criteria for OTL standards, several suggestions can be put forth. First, keep the particular uses to be made of the OTL standards in mind as criteria are developed. If OTL standards are to provide a vision of what excellent education can and should be for all students, such vision must be supported by research. Nothing could be worse than a new mechanism for promoting fads; education has had more than enough of those already. Further, if the vision is to inspire, then a criterion should be that OTL standards are uplifting and persuasive.

Second, in setting criteria for OTL standards, the appropriate degree of prescriptiveness must be decided upon. The choice is between OTL standards based on general principles that can guide practice and prescriptions that provide a script for practice. A prescriptive approach to OTL standards would result in a detailed list of dos and don'ts about what to teach, how to teach, and what resources must be available. This level of prescriptiveness is almost certainly not appropriate. A knowledge base to support such prescriptiveness is not available; a detailed formula for schooling that ensures students will learn simply does not exist. Research has, however, provided a great many principles that could serve to guide good instruction. Thus it would not be appropriate for OTL standards to specify the use of cooperative groups in instruction, though that strategy may be effective for some purposes. Meanwhile, research has made evident that instruction is far too passive. More worthwhile content would likely be learned if instruction were designed and delivered in ways that actively engage students with ideas, requiring that they communicate their thoughts to others and collect data to test their hypotheses.

Third, in constructing criteria for OTL standards, consideration should be given to the distinction between quantity and quality. Most state requirements concerning school inputs and procedures have been stated in terms of quantity. How many teachers are certified? How many courses are offered? How many students graduate? These indicators of quantity are far removed from what happens in instruction and from what students learn. If OTL standards are to point to directions for improved student learning, then they should consist of factors that are good predictors of student achievement. The focus should not be on what a teacher knows, but on how a teacher instructs. The focus should not be on whether good textbooks are available, but on how those textbooks are used to provide students access to worthwhile content. Money is a quantity, not a quality, indicator. The power of OTL standards will be increased to the extent they describe the quality of education as it is experienced by students.

Fourth, a parsimony versus complexity dimension exists to the problem of defining criteria for OTL standards. Education is an enormously complicated process; ethnographies have done much in recent years to uncover these complexities of teaching and learning. The question is whether OTL standards can reflect all of the complexities of education, and even if they could, would that complexity give OTL standards the power they need? I do not think so. For a vision to be persuasive, it must be understandable and accessible. For OTL indicators to provide information that people find useful and for them to be affordable, they must be focused on a few important aspects of education. It would be easy for OTL standards to get bogged down in trying to provide a rich and complete description of quality education. However, too much parsimony can lead to incomplete and misleading images and information that is misinterpreted. Criteria for OTL standards must establish the right balance between parsimony and complexity.

A fifth dimension for thinking through the problem of criteria for OTL standards is the distinction between content and pedagogy. For purposes of providing a vision or serving as a framework for indicators, both content and pedagogy should be included; but if OTL standards are to be used for school accountability, then they should focus on the content of instruction and not the pedagogical strategies employed to deliver instruction. First, descriptions of desired content of instruction flow directly out of the content standards being developed by professional societies and teachers. Greater clarity can be found about what content is wanted and how that relates to intended student outcomes than about what pedagogy is needed. Second, because the content of instruction can be considered a policy output of schools in its own right, content should not be determined by the professional judgment of an individual teacher. No such restrictions exist for pedagogy. Third, in a national probability sample of schools, A. Gamoran, A. C. Porter, and A. C. Gahng found that high school mathematics and science teachers' control over the content of their instruction had a slightly negative relationship with student achievement, while teachers' control over pedagogy had a positive relationship with achievement.[20]

An Example of Content OTL Standards

Without having some examples, seeing the potential of OTL standards can be difficult. One place where examples are available is in describing opportunities to learn high school math and science. In a 1994 study funded by the National Science Foundation, the question was examined of how increased standards in high school mathematics and science had affected the content of instruction that students received.[21] In particular, an effort was made to determine whether the increases in numbers of math and science courses required for graduation had led to a watering down of the curricula in those courses to accommodate the new influx of students. To investigate this question, data were collected in six states, twelve districts, and eighteen high schools serving high concentrations of students from low-income families. The focus of data collection was on the enacted curriculum in high school math and science courses, especially those that experienced big enrollment increases following state increases in graduation requirements. Interest in the enacted curriculum was at the heart of OTL standards.

To conduct the study, procedures were developed for measuring the content of high school mathematics and science instruction.[22]The first step was to develop a language for describing content—a language that, on the one hand, made sense to teachers and, on the other hand, was useful for mapping actual instruction against such templates as the NCTM *Content Standards* and the American Association for the

Advancement of Science's *Science for All Americans* calls for reform. The result was a four-dimensional language. The first two dimensions describe what comes to most people's minds when they think about the content of instruction. One dimension divided content up into large topical areas, for example in mathematics: number and number relations; arithmetic; measurement; algebra; geometry; trigonometry; statistics; probability; advanced algebra, precalculus, and calculus; finite and discrete mathematics. Similar large topical areas were identified for science. The second dimension subdivided the large topical areas into more precise descriptions of content. For example, within statistics, distinctions were made among collecting data, distributional shapes, central tendency, variability, correlation or regression, sampling, estimating parameters, and hypothesis testing. Thus the first two dimensions of the language describe, in two different degrees of detail, the nature of the material presented to students. A third dimension described the teacher's intended learner outcomes, distinguishing among memorizing, understanding concepts, data collection, comparing and estimating, performing procedures (for example, computations), solving routine problems and replicating experiments, interpreting data, solving novel problems, and building and revising theory. A fourth dimension distinguished modes of instruction: exposition, pictorial models, concrete models, equations and formulas, graphical work, lab work, and field work. Thus for any particular topic, such as linear equations in algebra, the four-dimensional language also specified the way in which the topic was presented and what about the topic students were to learn. For example, instruction might use equations and formulas to present linear equations in algebra, with the intention that students memorize the form of a linear equation.

The language for describing the content of mathematics and science instruction was used by teachers to complete daily logs on the content of their instruction in a particular section of a particular course for a full school year. Each week logs were mailed to a data collection site where they were reviewed, clarified when necessary, and then entered into an electronic data base. The log form asked teachers to describe up to five topics of instruction each day, specifying for each the four dimensions in the language and the degree of emphasis of that topic in the lesson. Emphasis codes were translated into instructional time and, by topic, were aggregated across lessons to provide descriptions of instruction for the full school year.

Independent classroom observations verified the validity of teacher logs. Teachers also completed retrospective questionnaires in which they were asked to provide information similar to that communicated through daily logs, and, for the subsample of teachers who provided both kinds of information, cross-validation of questionnaire data to log data showed promising results. Work is continuing to explore how the content language can be improved and how measurement strategies can be made more efficient. Daily logs are a labor-intensive measurement strategy that would be too expensive and cumbersome for OTL indicators; questionnaires might work well. Nevertheless, the data from the logs illustrate the potential power of OTL indicators.

Despite content of instruction being the single most powerful predictor of student achievement that is under the direct control of teachers, all too often the content of instruction is taken for granted.[23] The implications of taking content for granted can be illustrated by data from two teachers of physical science teaching in different states. Both teachers put heaviest emphasis in their instruction on physics, 58 percent and 57 percent of total instructional time (figure 3). One teacher spent almost 25 percent of instructional time on chemistry and 8 percent on general science topics, while the other teacher's emphases were just the opposite, 26 percent time on general science and only 14 percent on chemistry. The degree of alignment between the two teachers' instruction and an assessment of science achievement might differ, depending on the assessment's relative emphases on chemistry versus general science topics. Within the content area of physics, the more specific breakdown of topics taught was similar between the two teachers. Molecular and nuclear physics received virtually no attention, while the other possible topics received varying amounts of attention from 4 or 5 percent of total instructional time up to 10 percent.

The most interesting differences between the two teachers were found in their profiles on modes of instruction and learning outcomes. One teacher spent virtually all of the time lecturing and having students read materials (exposition), while the other teacher spent only 50 percent of instructional time on exposition, choosing instead to have a much richer profile of instructional strategies, including the use of pictorial models and lab work. Consistent with the differences between the two teachers on modes of instruction, the two teachers also differed sharply on what they intended for their students to learn. The teacher who emphasized exposition also emphasized memorization of facts as

FIGURE 3. *Instructional Time for Two Physical Science Teachers*

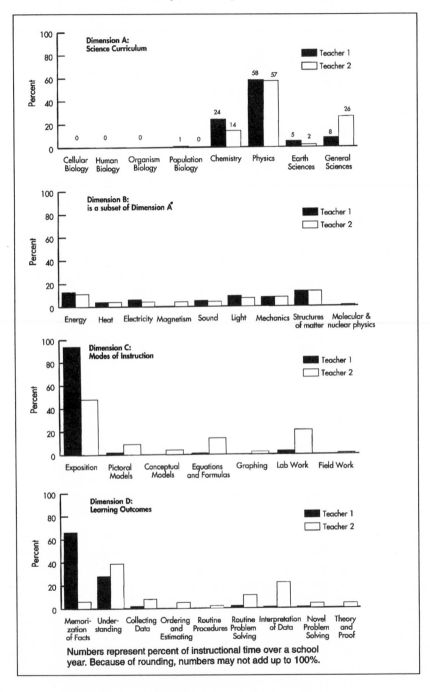

an intended outcome of instruction. The teacher who put a greater premium on use of pictorial and conceptual models and lab work strongly stressed understanding concepts, collecting and interpreting data, and being able to solve routine and novel problems.

Students taking physical science got sharply different instructional experiences, depending on which teacher they had. A transcript study would consider the two groups of students to have had the same physical science experiences. Also, the data make clear that one teacher provided instruction much more consistent with today's curriculum reforms than did the other. Today's science reforms seek instruction that is balanced between memorizing facts, on the one hand, and coming to understand concepts and to apply them, on the other.

Schools and teachers committed to improvement might find OTL indicator information such as that provided in figure 3 extremely useful. Teachers participating in the study were anxious to see their instructional profiles.

Most teachers do not feel apologetic about the content of their instruction even when discussing curriculum reform. Content profiles of teacher practices are easily mapped onto national professional content standards in ways that make clear where agreement exists and where it does not. Without such data, many teachers may fail to recognize ways in which their practices need to change if they were to come into alignment with today's curriculum reforms. Many teachers feel that their instruction already is roughly consistent with the curriculum reforms, despite findings in the study of high school math and science makes clear that their instruction is not. For example, across all teachers and courses studied, both mathematics and science were dominated by exposition, either verbal or written. In both subjects and for virtually all of the courses studied, students spent the majority of their time either being talked to by the teacher or working independently at their desks. In contrast, today's reforms call for a shift away from this picture of passive instruction and toward students' active engagement in the construction of their own knowledge. What little lab work that was done in mathematics was exclusively drill-and-practice at a computer terminal. In science, half the courses spent 5 percent or less of instructional time in lab work. In contrast, both math and science curriculum reforms of today call for a heavy emphasis on students' collecting and analyzing data and using real-world and lab-type experiences to present applications of concepts and skills.

The development of content indicators along the lines described here would represent a major step in moving discussions of opportunity to learn away from a predominant focus on quantity of instruction to something much more tightly tied to the quality of instruction. The language developed for the study of high school math and science has the flexibility to provide descriptions of quality in considerable detail, while it is also capable of being easily aggregated to parsimonious descriptions of content. For example, one can address the question of what fraction of time is spent on algebra in an algebra course that is required of all students (as opposed to such topics as arithmetic). At the same time, the language allows for description of exactly what kinds of algebra are covered, how they are covered, and with what intended learner outcomes.

CONCLUSION

Are OTL standards the answer to the age-old equity problems in U.S. schools? Should testing of student achievement with stakes for students be conditioned on a student's school first meeting OTL standards? Will OTL standards result in a new rash of litigation challenging the adequacy of education received by an individual (or group of individuals)? Will OTL standards lead to a standardization of education practice? The answers to these and similar questions appear to be no.

While the federal role in OTL standards does not appear to be headed toward heavy influence on what states will do, several states seem persuaded on their own to take OTL standards seriously. One source of information for predicting what states will do comes from the National Governors' Association work with California, New York, South Carolina, and Vermont. In developing the concept of OTL standards and how they might be used, all four states gravitated away from across-the-board school-by-school accountability. New York and South Carolina focused on the use of OTL standards in school self-analysis, with an emphasis on improvement. Vermont and California gravitated toward OTL standards in school-by-school reviews triggered by low student performance. OTL standards were seen as a resource for schools to draw on in their efforts to become more effective. Admittedly, these four states were responding to an NGA–sponsored competition for work on developing OTL standards; the directions of their work might not be predictive of more reluctant states. Some states are exploring the idea of creating something analogous to England's school inspection. There, a bureaucracy of some 475 inspectors has been created, with the goal of all twenty-seven thousand schools to be inspected once every four years.[24] Whether such externally imposed school inspections lead to school improvement and are worth their high cost remains to be seen. A Council of Chief State School Officers' survey of state rules and regulations concerning school inputs and processes revealed that most states believe they already have standards concerning OTL. This is a disappointing finding for those that hope OTL standards will serve as a mechanism for working with states to help strengthen their education systems.

The concept of OTL standards seems headed in the right direction. OTL standards are not going to become a major new form of school-by-school accountability. If they are to have any influence on school improvement, it will be through persuasion provided by visions of good education practice and information from OTL indicators on progress toward school improvement. Appropriately defined and used, OTL standards could play an important and much needed role in the standards reform movement. At least at this time, however, it appears as though leadership will not come from the federal level. States and professional organizations can and should do all in their power to provide clear visions of high quality education practice and indicator data that track school progress toward those visions.

NOTES

1. H. Rept. 103-446, *Congressional Record*, March 21, 1994, p. H1626.

2. *Debra P. v. Turlington*, 474 F. Supp. 244 (M.D. Fla. 1979); affirmed in part in 644 F.1d 397 (5th Cir. 1981).

3. National Council on Education Standards and Testing, *Raising Standards for American Education* (Washington, 1992); and University of Pittsburgh, Learning Research and Development Center, *The New Standards Project, 1992-95: A Proposal* (1992).

4. National Council of Teachers of Mathematics, *Curriculum and Evaluation Standards for School Mathematics* (Reston, Va., 1989); and F. J. Rutherford and A. Ahlgren, *Science for All Americans* (Oxford University Press, 1989).

5. National Governors' Association, *The Debate on Opportunity-to-Learn Standards: Supporting Works* (Washington, 1994).

6. H. Rept. 103-446, *Congressional Record*, p. H1631.

7. R. F. Elmore and S. H. Fuhrman, "Opportunity to Learn and the State Role in Education," in National Governors' Association, *The Debate on Opportunity-to-Learn Standards* (Washington, 1993), p. 87.

8. A. C. Porter, "School Delivery Standards," *Educational Researcher,* vol. 22, no. 5 (1993), pp. 24–30; and A. C. Porter, "Defining and Measuring Opportunity to Learn," in National Governors' Association, *The Debate on Opportunity-to-Learn Standards: Supporting Works,* pp. 33–72.

9. R. H. Meyer, "Can Schools Be Held Accountable for Good Performance? A Critique of Common Educational Performance Eduators," 1992.

10. R. F. Elmore and M. W. McLaughlin, *Steady Work: Policy, Practice, and the Reform of American Education* (Santa Monica, Calif.: RAND Corporation, 1988); and L. Darling-Hammond, "Creating Standards of Practice and Delivery for Learner-Centered Schools," *Stanford Law and Policy Review,* vol. 4 (1992), pp. 37–52.

11. G. F. Madaus and others, *The Influence of Testing on Teaching Math and Science in Grades 4–12,* NSF-SPA8954759 (Boston College, Center for the Study of Testing, Evaluation, and Educational Policy, 1992).

12. R. J. Shavelson and others, "Alternative Technologies for Large-Scale Science Assessment: Instrument on Education Reform," *School Effectiveness and School Improvement,* vol. 2, no. 2 (1991), pp. 97–114.

13. David Green, "Knowing Schools: The English Experience of School Inspection, 1983–93—Policies, Principles, and Practices Which Might Inform Education Reform in the USA," in National Governors' Association, *The Debate on Opportunity-to-Learn Standards: Supporting Works* (Washington, 1993), pp. 103–46.

14. National Council of Teachers of Mathematics, *Professional Standards for Teaching Mathematics* (Reston, Va., 1991).

15. E. Fennema, T. P. Carpenter, and P. L. Peterson, "Learning Mathematics with Understanding: Cognitively Guided Instruction," in J. E. Brophy, ed., *Advances in Research on Teaching,* vol. 1 (Greenwich, Conn.: JAI Press, 1989), pp. 195–222; and R. E. Slavin, N. L. Karweit, and N. A. Madden, *Effective Programs for Students at Risk* (Needham Heights, Mass.: Allyn and Bacon, 1989).

16. A. C. Porter, "Creating a System of School Process Indicators," *Educational Evaluation and Policy Analysis,* vol. 13, no. 1 (1991), pp. 13–29.

17. E. A. Hanushek, "When School Finance 'Reform' May Not Be a Good Policy," *Harvard Journal on Legislation,* vol. 28 (1991), pp. 423–56; and L. V. Hedges, R. D. Laine, and R. Greenwald, "Does Money Matter? A Meta-analysis of Studies of the Effects of Differential School Inputs on Student Outcomes," *Educational Researcher,* vol. 23, no. 3 (1994), pp. 5–14.

18. W. H. Clune, "The Shift from Equity to Adequacy in School Finance," *World and I,* vol. 8 (September 1993), pp. 389–405.

19. Jonathan Kozol, *Savage Inequalities: Children in America's Schools* (Crown, 1991).

20. A. Gamoran, A. C. Porter, and A. C. Gahng, "Teacher Empowerment: A Policy in Search of Theory and Evidence," in W. J. Fowler, B. Levin, and H. J. Walberg, eds., *Organizational Influences on Educational Productivity* (Greenwich, Conn.: JAI Press, forthcoming).

21. A. C. Porter, J. Smithson, and E. Osthoff, "Standard Setting as a Strategy for Upgrading High School Mathematics and Science," in R. F. Elmore and S. H. Fuhrman, eds., *The Governance of Curriculum: 1994 Yearbook of the Association for Supervision and Curriculum Development* (Alexandria, Va.: Association for Supervision and Curriculum Development, 1994), pp. 138–66.

22. Porter, "Defining and Measuring Opportunity to Learn."

23. W. H. Schmidt, "High School Course-Taking: A Study of Variation," *Journal of Curriculum Studies,* vol. 15, no. 2 (1983), pp. 167–82; and H. J. Walberg and T. Shanahan, "High School Effects on Individual Students," *Educational Researcher,* vol. 12, no. 7 (1983), pp. 4–9.

24. Green, "Knowing Schools."

Explaining Standards to the Public

The U.S. educational system is on the right track with standards and assessments, although many important questions still need to be addressed. Progress has been made since the six national education goals were announced and the National Education Goals Panel was formed. At that time, a recognition was made that goals could not be effectively measured without first reaching an understanding of what the goals and the authentic means of measurement are.

Having been a cochair of the National Council on Education Standards and Testing (NCEST), I think the panel did a good job of laying out the dimensions of the problem. Turning to the Goals 2000 legislation, I think that Congress and the Clinton administration did a good job of balancing the interests of the states and the federal government. But much more needs to be done to make the legislation effective.

When I first started working on these issues, I sought out the National School Boards Association. It was one of the first groups I wanted to speak to when I became chairman of NCEST because I anticipated that the fight over standards was going to be one of federalism and, at a state level, what was state and what was local. Such a strong tradition exists in the United States of local control of schools that I wanted to defang that argument so that discussions could be held on Theodore R. Sizer's question, "Who is the 'we' here?"

It is absolutely essential that "we" is consistently defined as the people of America. The people of America need to arrive at a conclusion about what a youngster should know and be able to do. Certain devices can be created to help them. One is the National Education Standards and Improvement Council (NESIC). Neither the Goals 2000 legislation nor the NESIC structural organization should suggest that the process used to determine what students should know be administered from the top down. The math standards prepared by the National Council of Teachers of Mathematics (NCTM), for example, were arrived at correctly, from the bottom up. They represent the best thinking in the country, collectively. My model for formulating standards has been: "Let's get the best thinking. Let's put it together. Let's take it out and get reaction and bring it back and take it out and bring it back." That is a continuous process.

Reflecting upon the discussion about standards, I want to come back to the initial statement of the problem; that is, people will become polarized on the federalism issue. That need not happen. Use the word *national* to mean "collaborative." I am on the street trying to enact this in policy and in practice.

In Colorado, fifteen hearings would be held on the draft standards. Colorado passed legislation calling for the development of model or voluntary standards at the state level, with each local district developing its own, which will "meet or exceed" the model standards. That is a careful use of words.

A committee was formed, which worked for several months. It wrote a first draft of standards and asked people for written comments. With a second, revised draft of the standards, it would hold public hearings. Imagine that you are a member of the committee and are going to Holyoke, Colorado, to ask a group of citizens about standards. One of the most important things that needs to be done is to find out how to communicate with people because the word *standard* is sometimes a barrier. When I am in Colorado, I try to explain what is meant by standards and what the goals are. I recently visited a TeleCommunication Incorporated (TCI) digitized facility, where TV signals are being digitized and put out into five hundred channels. I saw people at consoles, and I said, "What does a fourth grader need to know and be able to do in math to get that job?" I think that is a critical question for parents of America. They look at a job and say, "What does my youngster need to know and be able to do in the fourth grade in math to be on track to get that job?" That would be the first question I would pose in this series of hearings. Then I would say, "Look, we are talking about standards and assessments, and we are talking about what a youngster should know and be able to do."

I am a pilot, and I use that as an illustration. I say that a pilot needs to know and be able to do certain things. And they all understand that. Then I say, "It takes some people thirty-six hours to get a private license. It takes others forty-six hours to get a private license. But you have got to know certain things to get the license. They understand that people learn at different rates." Then I use a flip chart and draw the bell curve, and I ask, "How many of you want to ride with the pilot who is above average?" They all get confused. They do not know how to answer. Is it a trick question? I do not let them answer; I answer for them. I say, "I don't want to ride with a pilot who is above average. I want to ride with the pilot who knows how to fly the airplane." Then they say, "Oh, yes, I agree with that."

In those few sentences, I have gotten into standards. People understand that they do not want to ride with somebody who does not know how to fly the airplane. They do not want to have somebody operating on a heart who does not know how to operate on a heart. I help people recognize that you need to know certain things to get a good job and that educators want to teach children those things. Therefore, shouldn't the elements of this skill be identified, this element of citizenship, or whatever else is desired to try to set a standard for and measure?

Sometimes the idea of standards bothers people, and they ask, "Do you mean you are going to have everybody do the same thing?" They think that standards are not workable because students are different, with different abilities and different maturity. In response, I say, "Wait a minute, everybody can learn. But they are going to learn at different rates." Then they begin to buy into that, too. They say, "Okay, I am willing, Romer, to use this word *standard*. Standard is the content of my kid's education."

Going back to my pilot example, I point out what is fixed—what one needs to know—and what is variable—how long it takes to learn it. American schools reverse this. They say, "What is fixed is seat-time, and what is variable is what you know when you leave."

Other hurdles also exist. One of them is the potential problem of having the federal government tell the states what to do. Colorado is going to figure out its own standards, but it ought to learn from what the NCTM has already done in math, for example. Colorado should use the NCTM's work as a resource when writing its math standards. And it does.

Another controversial issue is outcome-based education (OBE). It must be hit head on. I propose saying, "Look, let's talk about what we are dealing with here. Come with me. Let's go out to TCI. Do you see those guys at that console? They have different ethnic and religious backgrounds. But they are all working on the same stuff, aren't they?" The answer is "Yes." I continue, "Well, can't we find a way that we can define what a youngster needs to know and be able to do in math in the fourth grade without getting caught up in a debate about outcome-based education and whether it will corrupt our values?" People say, "Yes, we can do that in math. But wait a minute. What about the values in history?"

I therefore feel that, as a strategy, math and science need to be moved on first. They are concrete. Now, as Sizer said, "rigor should be plural," and I agree. Even in math, more than one way can be used to describe or solve a problem. I am open to that argument. But there ought to be something that is so basic that Americans could get together on it. What does a youngster need to know and be able to do to be a functional citizen in employment and a functional citizen in a democracy and a functional citizen in the community? I do not think radically different descriptions will be found. The question should be approached with a sense of pluralism or plural rigors and without allowing the debate to be polarized by religious, sectarian, or federalism arguments.

I am struggling very hard in Colorado to say to people, "This is ours; this is yours; education reform has got to come from you from the bottom-up. But it is crazy for you to start from scratch. You ought to look at the best thinking in the country, and that is what we are trying to bring to you. It is crazy for you to start from scratch in each district; we ought to bring to you the best thinking in Colorado." In addition, some economies of scale are necessary when textbooks are published. Everybody cannot have an individual textbook for each district. People understand that.

What should be done to execute the present plans and policies under Goals 2000 or through individual state initiatives? First, I am very interested in people who can help communicate with the average parent. The National Academy of Sciences put out a pamphlet called "Measuring Up." It is a series of illustrations on fourth grade math. That has been the most effective pamphlet I have seen on standards because it says clearly—to parents, governors, and others—"Here is what we are talking about in fourth grade math. This is the kind of problem a youngster ought to be able to do."

Even better would be to do a specific exercise. I did this once at a governors' association meeting. I printed out a problem about how to measure up in math, and I said, "Let's work it together." The governors put the problem in their pocket when they left; they wanted to take it home. Communication techniques are needed that can be used with ordinary citizens and that can help them understand what the debate is about and get the ghosts out of the way. People with hands-on experience and commitment are needed to support this effort. In Colorado I worked with a group of legislators and others over a period of a year drafting a standards bill, and we got sufficiently together on it that we now can defend it on a bipartisan basis.

I believe that with the right kind of illustration, the right kind of language, differences can be sorted out and much that is shared can be found. Focus on what people have in common first. Deal with the core and begin to remove the polarization in debate over public education. Otherwise, a loss in the ability to communicate will result, as in the Englewood district in Colorado [where voters rejected school reforms].

Goals 2000 also ought not get caught up in the debate over federal mandates. All kinds of rumblings can be heard, and many state legislatures are passing resolutions about them. States are trying to organize constitutional conventions, for example. Goals 2000 should not be burdened with unfunded mandates. The discussion can be refocused. Talk about Goals 2000 can center on whether the legislation supports reform from the gound up.

Teachers need to be fully engaged and involved in the debate. Sizer had some insightful comments about needing to give teachers more than lists of things they have to teach.

Parents also need to be brought along. I had a conversation about education in Greeley, Colorado, with a group of twenty-one Hispanic parents. I was told, "Governor, we want vouchers. We do not believe that the dropout rate for our children will ever be cured unless we are in charge of their education." I responded, "No, I do not think that is right. I do not think you ought to leave the public education system, but I do think you ought to use charter schools and that you ought to work within the system with other parents and begin to create greater involvement by you as individuals and as leaders in your community about your children's education." That incident is an anecdotal illustration that a number of parents recognize the dire straits that public education is in and want to join to effect change. They need access to the debate and the dialogue about student learning.

If I were to predict, for Colorado, what group in the long term would be most effective in the systemic reform of education, I would put parents equal with teachers. The reason is that a large investment has been made in the current system, and both teachers and administrators are still caught up with the history of it. To help change the system, parents need access to the ongoing debate on standards and assessments.

I have been fascinated by the distinct roles played by the governor and the chief state school officer. I speak about this not because I am a governor, but because I am a student of politics and public policy. A governor is a person that the state generally looks to for a sense of priority, leadership, and organization, among other things. The chief state school officer has some of those elements, but in a more specialized function. Governors, however, come and go, while chief state school officers are more stable and permanent. Goals 2000 must have the support of political leadership for it to succeed.

The leadership at the federal level has a great history of micromanaging change. Federal education laws are proof of that. The federal role is limited in Goals 2000, which is good. Congress must be made to keep its hands off education in the future. Also, leadership must be developed at the state and local level, which means governors, state legislators, school board people, and teacher union officials.

As the law begins to be implemented, communication should not remain confined within the ranks of professional educators and chief state school officers. Local elected officials must be actively involved in the dialogue. One means to engage them is NESIC, which is a group that is going to develop the criteria by which reform is implemented. Some people who have run for office will need to be in the mix of NESIC, because a perspective of public policy implementation and communication is critical for success.

I agree with Marshall S. Smith and his outline of standards, assessments, professional development—changing the way in which the educational experience happens. Standards and assessments are the most hopeful, systemic tools to reshape American education. But competing for the attention of public officials will be a real challenge. Because I am one, I know how influential they can be.

The movement toward standards and assessments is one of my priorities. But I reached that conclusion only because I have been immersed in the issues. If others at various levels of government are to get involved—school boards, county and city offices, state legislatures, and governors—they also must get immersed. People are not going to buy into reform unless they are really into it; and once they get into it, they will make good decisions.

A war was waged recently in the West over grazing fees and land management. Each side was polarized. In Colorado four environmentalists and four ranchers eventually were brought together, with a couple of other people, and were asked to try to solve the problem. Interior Secretary Bruce Babbit also participated. The task was laborious. The ground rules stipulated that all decisions be unanimous. After eight weeks, a plan emerged about how to govern public lands and make decisions at a local level on grazing.

The Department of the Interior liked the plan so well that it was included as a model in new regulations. Ranchers and environmentalists in Colorado now work side by side because they fundamentally have the same values. How the ecological system is cared for within a drainage basin is going to dictate the economic, long-range vitality of cattle grazing. Ranchers know they have to live with this other world of users of public lands.

In the course of developing the plan, an agreement was reached to create local five-member committees including two environmentalists and two ranchers to make decisions about grazing. The question came up: What should be the residence requirement of the environmentalists? The environmental community said, "We have to have the right to have the person on a local committee in Gunderson, Colorado, be a resident of Maine because these are national lands." Wouldn't that argument blow any kind of compromise? But the group accepted that argument unanimously. Ranchers agreed because it had been decided that committee members could be residents anywhere so long as they know the territory, know the issues, and will commit themselves to a training session as a precondition to being on the committee.

In a very polarized circumstance, common agreement was found. The same can be done in education reform. Work hard on the religious right or the ones that say, "Local forever and never anything on the national basis." Get beyond the rhetorical ghosts and get down to the essential issue, which is: "If you want your son or daughter to hold that job at TCI, what do they need to know and be able to do?" Define the issue locally, as a local decisionmaking process that is being informed and facilitated by national opinion.

General Discussion

Diane Ravitch, as chairman and interlocutor of the panel, began by noting that Goals 2000 was enacted seven weeks earlier. The implementation of the complex law requires a vigorous national debate and discussion. To make the legislation comprehensible to Americans, people who understand the issues are going to have to talk about it wherever a crowd gathers to listen. Americans need to think hard about the kind of educational system they want and need.

Debate is needed, among other reasons, to counter a strong sense of complacency about educational achievement that has been documented repeatedly by polls. It also is needed to counter a growing backlash against standards that is taking place in many states and communities. Sometimes the backlash is associated with outcome-based education; people who oppose the state's imposition of values and socialization often end up opposing academic standards. In such situations, the fault is sometimes with the critics, who cannot tell the difference between what they call outcome-based education and what is actually academic standards. Just as often the fault lies with educators who prefer outcome-based education to academic standards. A backlash also has emerged against the idea that all children can learn. Some part of the public believes that the only way to ensure that all children learn is by holding all students back until the slowest child catches up. Rightly or wrongly, critics fear that the whole curriculum is going to be dumbed down. Further evidence of the backlash is a large and growing fear of performance assessment, fed by the notion that it means eliminating the standards supplied by objective testing.

There are additional aspects to the backlash against standards. In Ohio, for example, the U.S. Department of Education invoked the brand-new concept of opportunity-to-learn (OTL) standards to challenge the state's high school graduation standard. The state's graduation test is a minimum-competency test pegged to the ninth-grade level; students were given seven years' notice to prepare for that test.

The department's investigation raises serious questions about any state's ability to set meaningful content and performance standards, backed by a test.

Deborah Wadsworth reported that the Public Agenda Foundation has been documenting conversations about education reform almost since *A Nation at Risk* was published in 1983. A research organization, the foundation has been listening not only to the general public but also to groups all over the country that represent the educating professions, policymakers, and the business community. Recently parents and kids have been asked about education reform.

She said that Governor Roy Romer, better than anyone, would understand the fear of local discussion and of disagreement over local issues and that he was trying very hard to do something that has not been understood, which is to make a difference between publicizing reform or national standards and making the issue public.

The Public Agenda Foundation is engaged in new national research that is looking at the agenda of values discussion. Sensible, serious parents are raising very serious concerns about the standards' agenda. They may be manipulated by the religious right, but their concerns are very real. People raise questions, for example, about heterogeneous grouping.

The response of the expert community has been to assume the basest motives, that people are saying what they are saying because they do not want their kids educated with different kinds of kids or they do not want their kids' education dumbed down. However, people of every economic level and people of various races and ethnic backgrounds are saying: "I know from my own experience that kids need different kinds of settings, and they need different kinds of help, and for my kid, heterogeneous grouping does not work."

The experts listened to the public's concerns, checked them off, dismissed them, and moved on with their own agenda. It is happening all over the country. An unraveling of reform is taking place. Increasingly, very sensible middle-of-the-road people are very concerned about who the "we" is. They are very concerned about another issue that Theodore R. Sizer raised when he talked about teachers, the kind of reform de jour: "What are you doing to my kids? This is just more tinkering." They are very concerned about outcome-based education when, for them, that means that the schools are dealing with issues that they think the schools ought not to be dealing with. This needs to be confronted. The kind of public discussion called for by Governor Romer needs to be created, discussion that, outside of Colorado and a few other places, is not happening.

James Herbert from the National Endowment for the Humanities wanted to ask Marshall S. Smith about the quality of the performance and content standards as they have emerged or are emerging. The debate between systemic reform and civic discourse is interesting from a philosophical point of view. It is, however, a debate about procedure or a debate about constitutional arrangements and who should decide. Would it be a good idea if most of the classrooms in the United States were organized around some variation of these content standards and the kids were expected to learn these things? In answering, the case of the National Council of Teachers of Mathematics (NCTM) should be set aside because it developed outside this process in a different dynamic; other standards projects should be considered.

Smith pointed out that the question makes a lot of assumptions. One assumption is that a difference must exist between the civic discourse that Sizer talked about and the larger systemic reform strategy. No distinction should be made; the discourse must take place. Smith has written about the topic for a long time. He and Governor Romer pushed it when they served on the National Council on Education Standards and Testing, and Education Secretary Richard W. Riley believes in it. They admired Rick Mills's work as state superintendent in Vermont, which is not the approach that is built into Goals 2000. Mills himself could go to practically every school in Vermont and talk about the issues of assessment, student work, and standards and bring Vermont along. Vermont, like Colorado, is a difficult place because of its long history of local control and localism. That kind of experience has got to be replicated all over the country.

What can the federal government do to promote reform, apart from talk about it? Having the conversation is almost a contradiction because being said, at the same time, is, "This should not be a federal reform effort; this should be a state and local reform effort."

How can it be done? Problems have arisen, such as outcome-based education. An interesting coalition has formed. There is the question of tracking. The parents of gifted and talented kids, along with the religious right and others, for one reason or another, have heard one thing or another about some sort of standards movement and, perhaps, justifiably fear it because what they have heard is a fearsome thing.

Systemic reform and civic discourse have to work together. The one is not going to work without the other.

Smith made no comment on the quality of standards that are funded by the federal government. He said he was not familiar enough with them but knew that those projects have been reviewed in many cases and that they are moving along reasonably well.

Whether the National Education Standards and Improvement Council (NESIC) will decide if those particular projects will be the national voluntary standards remains uncertain. Also not certain is whether NESIC will decide if only one set of voluntary national standards would be set for mathematics. Two or three may emerge. NCTM is thought of as the standard of the standards. Perhaps it should be a voluntary national standard for mathematics decided by NESIC. But that is a decision that NESIC is going to have to make. Three or four years down the line, there may be competing national standards in mathematics, developed out of a small town in Colorado or by the state of California or South Carolina or Delaware or any of the other spots across the country that are developing standards that could build on what the NCTM did. The same thing could be done in geography, science, or anything else—build on national standards and the experiences of other countries and states.

Should standards be imposed in some way? Absolutely not. Will there be differences among the states and in some states among localities in the content standards and performance standards? Absolutely. Should they be of high quality according to a set of criteria that have to do with some sort of theory of the content and some sort of theory of human development and pedagogy? Absolutely. Should those be the kinds of criteria that NESIC applies? No, America should not have a monolithic single standard. Will this make it very hard to have a national test that meets the double criteria of being a decent thermometer and testing to what is taught in schools? Absolutely. That is a fundamental problem that will have to be lived with for decades.

Smith said that Sizer took a strategic approach by suggesting that standards exist only for the three Rs. It is not obvious that at least one of the Rs is noncontroversial. There may even be two strategies for writing, two different ways of thinking about two different conceptions. So, everything is going to be controversial and should be, which comes back to the notion that public discourse is necessary and that it has to be very powerful.

Eugenia Kemble of the American Federation of Teachers (AFT) spoke to the references made in the conference to teacher cynicism and teachers being part of the problem.

The AFT commissioned an internal poll by Peter Hart, an independent pollster. The results indicated, first, that the top concern among teachers is parent involvement in student discipline, and, second, that teachers are very willing to reform themselves and they see themselves as needing that. The pollster read three statements and asked the respondent to choose the one that best describes his or her teaching skills. Fifty percent picked "With more support and training I could still improve my teaching a great deal"; 36 percent, "I could improve my teaching somewhat but probably not a great deal." That is, 86 percent of teachers feel that they could improve their skill.

A series of questions also were posed. "Thinking about your school today, would you say that the academic standards for students are too high or too low or are about right?" The response was: too high, 4 percent; too low, 51 percent; about right, 43 percent. Because controversy has arisen over whether the United States should be looking at foreign systems, poll participants were asked: "Compared with the students in Europe and Japan, would you say that American students, generally, achieve academically at a lower level, at about the same level, or at a higher level?" The response was lower level, 71 percent, and about the same, 15 percent. "In your opinion is it important that the United States have academic standards as high as those in Europe and Japan, or is it not really that important as long as we are satisfied with our standards?" Sixty-three percent said it is important to have standards as high as Europe and Japan. It is noteworthy that more than half of the sample is urban teachers. "There is now a proposal to establish rigorous world class educational standards that would define what a student is expected to know and be able to do at different grade levels: In general, would you say such standards are a good idea or not a good idea? Do you feel strongly about this or not strongly about this?" Sixty-eight percent think standards are a good idea; 47 percent felt strongly and 21 percent did not feel strongly. "Here are some reasons people have given for supporting a system of standards. For each one please indicate agree, strongly agree, somewhat agree," and so on. The highest rating, 82 percent agree, either strongly or somewhat, with this point; "You only get what you ask for, and we have not asked enough of students. If we set high standards and teach to them, achievement will go up."

A collection of responses on standards and concerns about standards was presented. The highest among positives on standards was: "Everyone should be equal. If everyone is getting the same education, the results will be more equal." The lowest for the negative concerns among standards was that they should be local and that each individual school system should decide for itself.

Ravitch added that, in the research done for a New Standards Project, parents were asked to think about the differences between American schools and foreign systems, specifically, Japan and Germany. They responded, "Don't talk to me about Japan. All these Japanese kids are killing themselves." Then they were asked to compare the U.S. schools with Sweden; the response was, "Don't compare our kids to Japan; they are all killing themselves." Meanwhile, the suicide rate is higher for American kids than for Japanese kids.

Shirley Malcom, of the American Association for the Advancement of Science, maintained that, to a certain extent, reform-minded educators still tend to talk past each other. Not everyone is talking about the same thing when talking about standards. The issue of standards should be dealt with on a conceptual level, instead of concentrating on the details, so that the whole question about curriculum can be bypassed. But still, when people talk about standards, they are at a grain-size that is very different.

Another problem is the lack of a definition for what constitutes a system. Talk is heard about alignment across different parts of the system, but nothing is being said about the arts and sciences faculty. If higher education is not brought into the discussion on the arts and sciences side, what is done is not going to matter.

And there is the whole question about the culture of the community. Yet to be determined is what eduators want parents to do, whether they are to be brought around to the education side or whether positive pro-active strategies should be engaged to make them a part of the solution. Not a great deal of intellectual investment has been made in looking at exemplary strategies for parental involvement and figuring out how parents can be helped not only to understand what the reform means, but also to assume a positive role in supporting what will be necessary in their own communities. Public involvement does not equal community of learners.

Educators also are talking past each other with regard to romanticizing what teachers are able to do. At some point, they run out of their knowledge base, and only a partnering of teachers and scholars will bring success. This kind of middle-ground discussion does not take place, however.

Cities also need to be the focus of some attention; they are very different in many cases from the states in which they are embedded. Their problems are more severe, and they may require a decoupling, such as has been done with the National Science Foundation's urban systemic programs, to deal with some of the deeply rooted problems. More people need to get involved. Educators are not the only ones that need to be in this conversation. Educators can positively involve people from community-based organizations and ministers in supporting the whole notion of reform.

The issue of entitlement versus competitive forms of grant making at the federal level also needs to be addressed. On the one hand, a model exists in which everyone gets a check for whatever they choose to do; on the other, a model exists in which applicants compete and the money goes only to those who know what they are going to do with it. Educators need to figure out how to give money in such a way as to have maximum leverage.

Talk can revolve around theory, but the rubber meets the road in implementation. How can theory, practice, and research be brought together to affect culture? Is there a culture for learning? Is there a culture that supports reform? Which actions will truly affect that culture?

Ravitch noted that Shirley Malcom headed a committee that created one of the best documents on the standards issue. It is called *Promises to Keep: Creating High Standards for American Students* and was prepared for the National Education Goals Panel. Ravitch also said that Ramon Cortines, the chancellor of the New York City Board of Education, has been trying to bring the discussion about standards to that city. He established a broad-based group to create curriculum frameworks for the public schools and announced that all students would be required to take advanced courses in mathematics and science. Every time he goes out to talk about standards, the people who are most eager to support him are parents, because they fear that other children are getting a good education and their children are not. He is finding tremendous popular support at the local level for the kind of reform that Eugenia Kemble described.

Peter Smith, of the George Washington University, asked if it is fair to say that policymakers, scholars, and governmental figures at the

state and the federal level have to be in a variety of support positions—supply context knowledge, draft standards—but that the fundamental power and control to create learning environments and
expectations for teaching and learning have to reside with teachers,
parents, and children who construct learning?

Smith said that Sizer described a contrast between a historic discourse and the more modern and technological discourse. An
immutable chemistry exists among three constituencies: the people
whose professional lives are affected every day, the children whose
lives are subjected to schooling every day, and parents who only have
a limited number of children to care about. Entrusting to parents the
power that goes with being at the center of the debate and the risk taking means that educators must arrogate for themselves a secondary,
but important, role. If educators cannot do that, they will continue to
talk past each other and fail at developing and inventing new schools.

Roy Romer agreed with Peter Smith but did not think the argument
should be defined as either/or. In the illustration involving grazing,
the decisionmaking was forced down to the lowest common level and
the assumption was that those who are doing the grazing ought to
make policy about it. But the world does not work that way. The world
works with legislation, bureaucrats, executive departments, field
agents representing bureaucrats, and environmentalists. It is the same
with education.

Those who are making policy in education and who are political
must have a world view and the good sense to construct an appropriate structure for success. Not to be forgotten, however, is that school
board elections occur; school board members change and they will
throw out what they do not like. So, everyone must be brought along,
while recognizing the importance of leadership and policy.

Basil Whiting, from Public/Private Ventures, commented that he
comes to the discussion with a fair amount of experience consulting in
industry. He added that much of what was said at the conference
echoes the kind of things that have gone on in the board rooms of
industry since the mid-1970s, as large national corporations—competing in an international market—have had to transform themselves
from bureaucratic, hierarchical, controlling organizations into flatter,
leaner, nonbureaucratic organizations that are nimble and quick, prepared to rely upon the creativity of the front-line person. They have
done it, in part, through the systemic change approach that Marshall

Smith talked about, through using goals, visions, assessments, and so on. Thus far it has not resulted in a Tayloristic, controlling, and ossified workplace. Instead, it has unleashed freedom, creativity, and effectiveness. Isn't there something to be learned from the industrial experience, as that sector of the economy has tried to accommodate to a world market?

Sizer responded by saying educators should attend to it but not too much because of the nature of schooling, which is ultimately about kids' minds and hearts. The product, therefore, is not as easily defined as it is in the industrial area. It is just apples and oranges in that respect; it is not anything more than that. That is a fundamental difference. Further, educators are dealing with a public service, a public profession. Considerable attention should be paid to things such as social work, public safety, and the work of police departments. Society should attend to the delivery of public services that appear to work, as attentively as in the industrial sector.

Andrew C. Porter added that much more is known about what to do with schools, teachers, and students who are all convinced that they can get better on the systemic reform agenda, but not much about what to do for schools, teachers, and students who do not have that agenda and are not convinced. Not a lot has been said about how to turn that around.

Ramsay Selden, with the Council of Chief State School Offiers, wanted to pursue the question of whether there is a problem with standards being conceived of as universal or general when, as Sizer observed, learning is, by its nature, very personal, very idiosyncratic to kids. Learning is a combination of things that are personal and idiosyncratic to people but also universal, so that, as Governor Romer noted, people can be prepared to go work in good jobs at a computer plant.

But in terms of the premise of standards structuring the system and the premise of schools needing to be organized at the street level, the question becomes: Is it possible to formulate standards and not have them be seen as things that are inappropriately general so that they conflict with the extent to which things have to be personal or idiosyncratic at the level of the school with the child?

Romer referred to a debate taking place in Colorado over literature. Who should devise the booklist? Somebody is going to make that decision. Perhaps a public discussion should be started to determine what the community believes are the great works of literature that people ought to read in certain age groupings. The discussion could be broad enough to include a whole lot of different points of view, but whether standards should have booklists remains unanswered.

How would this public discussion get going? Great debates were held in the early days of the National Education Goals Panel. Blood was all over the floor. It was great television. People throughout the country still say: "Yeah, we saw that back then." The debate that has been raised with the religious right and the others needs to be reconvened, in a constructive way. It ought not be done with a "he-said-you-said" polarizing approach.

Romer did not see a contradiction. If teachers, parents, and kids were brought together to talk about the curriculum, they would find much in common—on content, strategies, and a variety of things that they all believe that kids should know and be able to do. They may approach things in different ways, but that is not a contradiction. They may structure the schools in very different ways. The trick is to be able to think about this discussion not as specifying things on a detailed level, and not as specifying things even by a year, but across a period of time that makes sense educationally and makes sense to parents and teachers.

The bottom line is that all of the extreme positions are wrong. Everything in moderation is probably okay. But quality must be put at the top. Good education is the goal. A particular pedagogical style should not be emphasized. Much is known about reading. Only phonics cannot be taught to everybody, and only whole language cannot be taught to everybody, with the expectation of having a nation of readers. Teachers must be free to use their professional judgment. Professional judgment is important all the way through this process.

Decades will be needed to begin to approach any of the reform visions. But there are common elements, common sets of ideas, on which most would agree. In the long run, fundamental agreements can be reached among the people who are trying to think this thing through.

DONALD M. STEWART

Holding onto Norms in a Sea of Criteria

The tale of the young George Washington, it is said, offers an early insight into the American culture. Truth-telling morality notwithstanding, Washington received an axe, not a book nor even a curricular guide, before his swift and fateful encounter with that cherry tree. From carving out an inhabited wilderness 350 years ago to building a school system for the burgeoning urban masses at the start of the twentieth century, Americans have prized practical efficiency, a cool pragmatism, increasingly accompanied by the fair handmaiden of science. During the first decades of the twentieth century, many early school bureaucrats, whom historian David B. Tyack has called the "administrative progressives," saw the uniform curriculum, poorly trained teachers, dull recitation methods, and the undifferentiated structure as "rigid, unscientific, wasteful, and inhumane." Admiring imitators of a rising business class, the early bureaucrats were "evangelists for new educational goals of science and social efficiency. They . . . wanted a one-best system but it was to be a more complex, differentiated organization adapted to new social and economic conditions."[1] Supportive of the pedagogical innovators who advocated the "project method" or "activity curriculum," they sought to individualize instruction, to meet the different needs of different children, and to prepare them efficiently for their likely work after school. Any desire for the vague liberal education of an earlier era was so much wistful idealist longing; tough social conditions, a dramatically changing international economy, and a large influx of the children of immigrants demanded that the school system adapt efficiently.

Not surprisingly, some found the efficiency emphasis a bit debilitating. They questioned what seemed an overly mechanical sense of education, as an indication of a certain spiritual dryness and narrowness. Was it not a caricature of life, created by the modern scientistic culture, where confidence in the person has been replaced by confidence in a method, the cool delivery of a new product called curriculum, the seamless placement of human capital into the national production system? As the school board president of Middletown wryly put it in the 1920s: "For a long time all boys were trained to be President. Then for a while we trained them all to be professional men. Now we are training boys to get jobs."[2] Or as Brown University president Vartan Gregorian has asked: Have Americans simply come to value education for what it will give them and not what it will make of them?[3]

Discrediting this emphasis on social efficiency is too easy. Members of large organizations appreciate those with the practical skills of operations. Schools of the 1930s, for example, were facing a student population that had doubled during the previous decade; far greater percentages entered school and stayed in school longer. Taxpayers rightfully demanded a clear accountability for dollars spent. Most teachers and administrators sought, armed with the educational science of their day, to individualize education efficiently; ironically, their methods were later bemoaned as impersonal categorization by those championing similar ends.

The Scottish political scientist D. W. Brogan identified a second major historical theme—the strong element of religious enthusiasm and salvational hope attached to American schools. He often enjoyed referring to the American public school as "the formally unestablished national church of the United States."[4] Using the Book of Hebrews' definition of faith as a belief in what one cannot see and a hope in things to come, Americans from the early colonists onward have sought to advance the American soul through schooling, whether in formally religious or secular terms. With missionary zeal, early settlers such as the Rev. John White saw in education the chance to combat that large portion of colonists who were "a multitude of rude ungovernable persons, the very scum of the land."[5] Schools spread to the Wild West, and later to inner-city denizens, seeking not only to spread literacy but also to stand firm against the moral anarchy that threatened the American spirit on those frontiers. So strong is this tendency in American history, claims historian William McLoughlin, that "American history is . . . best understood as a millenarian movement."[6] Recall that Americans recently made a bestseller of a book claiming the closing of the American mind by explaining "how higher education . . . failed democracy and impoverished the souls of today's students."[7]

This salvational or faith aspect of U.S. educational history is often known by the sheer irrelevance of empirical data to its claims. Positions are staked out for the intrinsic merit of their moral values, or their capacity to transform the American soul, to make it more righteous, cooperative, orderly, socially acceptable, or even politically correct. School reforms often share in this tradition by their rhetorical flourish; the past is always a sinful one, requiring a conversion of heart and mind, a rededication to first principles, with the inevitable promise of pedagogical heaven to follow the sacrifice and pain. The camp meeting appeal is often enhanced by use of unassailable terms, such as "coherent" and "systemic," those most currently in vogue. Who wished not to be "progressive"? Who can oppose authenticity, deep understanding, real performance, or any curriculum that promises to be the "pacesetter"?

The purpose of highlighting these tendencies is not to caricature them; they continue to greatly benefit American schooling. Without a certain religious fervor and pragmatic efficiency, many of the best innovations might remain pipe dreams. Many of the finest educators embody these tendencies. And many of the best current calls for reform participate in these broad traditions. The danger arises when a reform draws from an unbalanced mixture of these two complementary elements. Reform becomes reckless when its promises avoid all possibility of empirical proof or only smooth the wheels of a cold but technically efficient instructional delivery system. Reform becomes reckless when it presumes that these two tendencies inevitably oppose each other, form extreme poles along an educational spectrum, and offer irreconcilably different paths of reform.

For even with the considerable skepticism, even cynicism, among many school people and their communities, the public at large remains susceptible to school reforms that tap the rhetorical appeal of either efficiency or salvation or both. School reform continues to be touted as critical to national economic efficiency, even though economists have failed to establish successful schooling for all as a major variable in an economy's international competitiveness. Many still promote unproven assessments based upon unproven premises that promise a pedagogical conversion to classroom teachers. Some still argue that tough real-world criterion-referenced exams will guard against wimpy relativist norm-referenced exams, even though the designation has more to do with how the scores are reported than the fundamental nature of the exams. Norm-referenced exams have criteria behind them, and criterion-referenced exams can be normed. And others still insist that the primary, and at times seemingly sole, priority of schooling is to efficiently sort out and develop human capital in a seamless and perhaps colorless educational production system from early walkers to briefcase bearers.

A sign of imbalance among these twin tendencies is the fight against phantom enemies and the heralding of mythic champions. Because few will oppose efficiency or some sort of salvation, a reliance upon just one of these themes must create a phantom enemy. A concrete example is test format and content; in particular, that often misunderstood assessment, the Scholastic Aptitude Test (SAT).

According to some enthusiasts, a standardized test such as the SAT, especially those questions that are in multiple-choice format, only tests low levels of thinking and is to blame for narrow and stagnant learning environments in classrooms, forcing an emphasis on superficial coverage of fragmented knowledge. The slayer of these dragons will be performance assessments, authentic assessments, portfolios, and a general avoidance of independently developed curriculum-neutral assessment instruments for whatever purpose.

Some standardized, multiple-choice tests, especially those given in early years and with high stakes, do not support the kind of teaching and learning endorsed now. Yet fervor often allows no distinctions. The SAT, believe it or not, tests higher levels of thinking, and this is not a recent phenomenon. A 1963 research report from the Test Development Division of the Educational Testing Service aimed to "dispel a myth: the myth of the multiple-choice question as superficial exercise—one that requires little thought, less insight, and no understanding."[8] The report then analyzed twenty-two sample questions to make its point clear. A 1994 analysis of SAT I math questions found that they provided a valid measurement of the National Council of Teachers of Mathematics (NCTM) *Curriculum Standards* themes of problem solving and reasoning abilities, and a reasonable bearing on the new mathematical connections theme.[9] Another 1994 study found that some twenty questions validly assessed the higher-level thinking skills of analysis and problem solving, using Benjamin Bloom's cognitive taxonomy.[10]

In terms of the SAT's relationship to the "new" conceptions of active learning and deep understanding in schools—conceptions that Linda Darling-Hammond reported "are virtually identical to those of the Progressives at the turn of the [twentieth] century, in the 1930s, and again in the 1960s"—the claim that supposedly decontextualized testing restricts good pedagogy must be addressed.[11] First, remember that all testing is, to some degree, decontextualized, and it is always but a small sample of a learner's behavior. Unless a device is implanted in a child's head to monitor his or her thoughts twenty-four hours a day, that problem will remain. Second, the relative strength of an assessment's format on a teacher's pedagogy has perhaps been seriously overstated. Recent research by University of California at Los Angeles, Center for Research on Evolution, Standards, and Student Testing researchers Audrey J. Noble and Mary Lee Smith, evaluating the lack of changes in classrooms after a high-stakes performance-based assessment was put in place in Arizona, suggested that using new assessments to drive curriculum and instructional reform may be problematic.[12]

Finally, to effectively assess thinking, including higher orders of thinking, three things are required: (1) a theory of the domain being tested; (2) a model of the learner, especially the "expert" learner; and (3) a theory for how to move learners to more expert levels.[13] All three of these do not exist to a great degree in many domains. Well-structured domains, such as in mathematics and science, allow a better chance to assess more complex thinking. In messier domains, such as history or literature, not enough understanding has been reached of the various structures to completely assess the complexity of thought, especially if any stakes are attached to the results, high or low. These clear technical constraints are one reason states are rightly refusing to rush into new assessments, according to a 1994 report by the National Education Association and the Council for Educational Development and Research.[14] And, to avoid educational hubris, a recognition must be made that many of the finest educational ambitions for U.S. students may always involve, as Eliott W. Eisner put it, "forms of performance for which the pre-definition of outcomes cannot be specified."[15]

Exciting advances in measurement, and in psychology's understanding of cognitive processes, are prompting exploration of new and innovative means of assessment, motivated by a well-balanced mix of fervor and practicality. And as instructional feedback, good teachers have always used a wide variety of loosely constructed and creative means of assessing students, and their experimentation usefully informs measurement research. There is nothing sacred or ultimately efficient about the multiple-choice format, and in collaboration with the Educational Testing Service (ETS), for example, the College Board is involved in extensive research and development in computer-adaptive assessments. The new SAT I, offered for the first time in March 1994, already incorporates student-constructed responses in the math section and a greater reliance on reading passages in the verbal. To some these changes were dramatic; to others, a far cry from the measurement Valhalla they seek. But, when dealing with the lives of the young, advances must be made cautiously upon the back of solid and extensive research, prudently avoiding the rushed or intemperate reform, choosing to serve students over waving the banner of salvation or efficiency. If only to teach by example, intellectual honesty must be modeled in the standards and assessments.

Another sign of an imbalanced tendency toward religious fervor or efficiency obsession can be found in the avoidance by some reformers of the wider ecology of testing. The device becomes the magic key, to the clouds or to the engine room. But tests happen in larger systems of schooling, within the larger societal context, and are ignored at society's peril.

A myopic concentration on the nature of the assessment device, for example, can obscure the way that device may frustrate broader educational aims. Take the desire by a few to make tightly linked curriculum-specific tests the sole criterion for both high school graduation and university admission, a magical seamless efficiency. What happens to the ability of curriculum-neutral tests, such as the Preliminary Standard Aptitude Test (PSAT) or SAT, to provide opportunities to students who have overcome weak curricula in their schools? How can hope be held out to those valiant students who—often with the support of family, local churches, community organizations, and even neighborhood libraries—develop themselves in spite of the lack of equitable academic preparation provided by their schools? Will they hear the wonders of such narrow standards over the din of crashing hopes? Can the United States afford to have its system of assessments send the signal that only what is learned in school courses counts? Shouldn't the system of assessments say clearly to students of varying school backgrounds, or to students seeking second chances, or to students reentering the educational pipeline from a nontraditional portal, that the ability to reason well across disciplines, the ability to learn however or wherever gained, also counts for a great deal?

In a time when the schools face increasing numbers of immigrant children, a great enthusiasm has arisen for more testing. Can a new, improved assessment design ensure against the abuses attributed to earlier eras?

In a time when public schooling as an institution faces an increased challenge from commercialization, from those who would privatize public schooling into the delivery of educational services, do federally inspired standards and assessments not facilitate such a process?

And in a time of tight government budgets, a lackluster economy, and the inevitable unevenness of a long educational reform effort, the preference for political prescription, that most deceptive ally, has nudged its nose under the big tent. Unlike the internally developed and consensus-driven process that produced the widely accepted NCTM standards, most disciplinary groups have had to respond to an externally driven, politically prescribed standard-setting process. What has emerged is a set of stand-alone standards, lacking a shared purpose and coherence, and requiring an extension of the human life span for their completion. Their top-down creation promises limited acceptance by most classroom professionals. Teachers cannot be told, on the one hand, "go and create thoughtful, active learning environments that tap the essential questions of your students' lives," and, on the other, "oh, by the way, here's a list of what all that will mean to you."

While sincerely applauding the federal government's efforts to establish broad political support for both equity and excellence, the College Board remains concerned that government actions not transform academic matters into political ones. Such a historically unprecedented intrusion threatens both the integrity of academic standards and the vitality of any reform it attempts to impose. For to develop academic standards outside of communities of learning and then mandate their usage is, as C. S. Lewis phrased it in another context, to "remove the organ and demand the function . . . [to] castrate and bid the geldings be fruitful."[16]

To avoid this end, the board has been proud to cosponsor, along with six national subject-matter organizations, the Forum on Standards and Learning, a cross-associational operational alliance, deeply embedded in the academic and teaching community of the United States. Building upon the board's long history of collaborative school-college academic standard-setting, including a decade of experience with Project EQuality and the famed "green book," *Academic Preparation for College*, the forum also taps the collective expertise of some 280,000 teachers across the United States. The forum provides a historically critical vehicle of support for academic standard-setting that can address questions of overall purpose, that can illuminate common and connecting principles of learning across subject areas, and that can promote the generative, rather than prescriptive, nature of standards in contributing to the professional growth of teachers and other educational practitioners. Instead of building upon a mistrust of practitioners, the board is shoring up the means for their constant involvement with standards that will require continual revision. By promoting the generative nature of academic standards, the board recognizes the wider ecology of standards and assessments and thus hopes to build the broad consensus among teachers that remains the foundation of any sustained and successful reform.

Recognizing the themes of science-based efficiency and belief-based fervor, how might the twin American tendencies be balanced in the current debate? Where should beliefs be invested, and where should the effort be made to better apply science to educational efficiency? Three brief points need to be considered.

In terms of efficiency, an opportunity exists today to take advantage of phenomenal advances in the technologies of communication, and these promise to provide as seamless a logistical transition between school and college as students have ever experienced and a rich multidirectional and cross-sector dialogue about education among teachers, students, researchers, professors, and the wider public. These technologies offer historically unparalleled and potentially broad access to educational resources for U.S. citizens. The growth in Internet participation alone promises both increased educational resources and enriched consensus building concerning academic standards.

Beyond efficiency, religious fervor could be applied to at least two areas in such a manner as to put the tireless circuit-riding preachers to shame. First, educators—and educators as citizens—must boldly preach to all who will listen that the outrageous inequities that tear at the nation's body politic as any chronic and debilitating disease cannot be accepted. With apologies to the handgun control folks, tests do not sort people, people do. Long before schools have the chance to sort and track in the insidious ways that they sometimes do, long before the student enters a classroom of active or passive learning, long before a student is put into a dead-end curricular track, society sorts and tracks large segments of its population into dead-end lives and desperate communities. No hiding is allowed behind the promises of a new assessment format, a new set of standards, a new set of structures—or behind the robes of judges to bring about reasonable opportunities for youth. Educators cannot stand by idly as need-based aid is weakened and only give polite lip service to the equal opportunity to learn for every citizen. When an estimated 76 percent of high-income students complete their bachelors degrees versus 4 percent of their low-income classmates, educators cannot stand by silently or shrug off the responsibility because the problem is wider than the classroom.[17]

Finally, faith must be reasserted in the principle of institutional autonomy through an encouragement of internally derived institutional aims, on both collegiate and precollegiate levels. As Carnegie Foundation president Ernest Boyer noted for higher education, ironically the aims for postsecondary schooling have narrowed just as access to it has expanded. In an era when commercial and governmental forces stand more than willing to define the ends the school and academy are meant to serve, efforts to raise standards will ultimately fail if the capacity of institutions to engage in mission-driven reform are not preserved and enhanced. Academic freedom and institutional autonomy remain the ultimate basis for world class educational standards and the true preserve of a rich diversity of excellence.

David K. Cohen and Michael S. Garet stated twenty years ago that educational policy must be read for the "grand story" it embodies about the nature of education and its vision of society.[18] Educators need to reinvigorate discussion of school reform and move it beyond a debate about false dualisms, phantom enemies and triumphant saviors. Schools need to be built up as communities of learners, not passive recipients of externally created ends.

To do this, democracy must be seriously affirmed at local community levels, and remember that, as Coalition of Essential Schools chairman Theodore R. Sizer said, "those who assert that 'the people' can never be trusted with setting standards sing an arrogant and dangerous tune."[19] As psychologist Sigmund Koch urged in a reference to the state of psychology, "intellectual finitude" must be faced, and that at times "the false hubris with which we have contained our existential anguish in a terrifying age has led us to prefer easy yet grandiose pseudoknowledge to the hard and spare fruit that is knowledge."[20] And a choice must be made, finally and firmly, to take science's deliberate efficiency and democracy's profound faith seriously. Both demand the discipline of their methods and call for a profound commitment to constructing the shared ends of a common human destiny. For in the complex web of human relationships that shapes what is called teaching, no list of federal standards, no efficient Internet listserver, and no list of assessment questions will provide sufficient hiding space from the judgment of history on the outrageous educational inequities that are allowed to persist and that demand no less than the most earnest religious fervor to rectify.

NOTES

1. David B. Tyack, *The One Best System: A History of American Urban Education* (Harvard University Press, 1974), p. 188; and R. E. Callahan, *Education and the Cult of Efficiency: A Study of the Social Forces That Have Shaped the Administration of the Public Schools* (University of Chicago Press, 1962).

2. Robert S. Lynd and Helen Merrell Lynd, *Middletown: A Study in Contemporary American Culture* (New York: Harcourt, Brace & Co., 1929), in M. Lazerson, ed., *American Education in the Twentieth Century: A Documentary History* (New York: Teachers College Press, 1987), p. 89.

3. Bill Moyers, ed., *A World of Ideas: Conversations with Thoughtful Men and Women about American Life Today and the Ideas Shaping Our Future* (Doubleday, 1989), p. 185.

4. D. W. Brogan, *The American Character* (Knopf, 1944), p. 137.

5. P. L. Ford, ed., *The New-England Primer* (Columbia University, Teachers College, 1987 and 1962), p. 52.

6. W. G. McLoughlin, *Revivals, Awakenings, and Reform: An Essay on Religion and Social Change in America, 1607-1977* (University of Chicago Press, 1978).

7. Allan Bloom, *The Closing of the American Mind: How Higher Education Has Failed Democracy and Impoverished the Souls of Today's Students* (Simon and Schuster, 1987).

8. T. D. Division, *Multiple-Choice Questions: A Close Look* (Princeton, N.J.: Educational Testing Service, 1963). My thanks to John Fremer for this reference.

9. R. L. Linn, *The Educational Reform Agenda: Assessment, Standards, and the SAT,* report for the Trustees, Research and Development Committee (Princeton, N.J.: College Board, 1994).

10. Conversation with Howard Everson, May 3, 1994.

11. Linda Darling-Hammond, "Reframing the School Reform Agenda: Developing Capacity for School Transformation," *Phi Delta Kappan,* vol. 74 (1993), pp. 752–61; cited in R. Glaser and E. Silver, "Assessment, Testing, and Instruction: Retrospect and Prospect," in Linda Darling-Hammond, ed., *Review of Research in Education* (Washington: American Educational Research Association, 1994), pp. 393–419.

12. Audrey J. Noble and Mary Lee Smith, *Measurement-Driven Reform: The More Things Change, the More They Stay the Same,* CRESST/CSE technical report no. 373 (University of California at Los Angeles, Center for Research and Evaluation, Standards, and Student Testing, 1994).

13. Personal communication from John Fremer, May 6, 1994.

14. L. Bond, *Surveying the Landscape of State Educational Assessment Programs* (Council for Educational Development and Research and National Education Association, 1994), p. 4–5.

15. Eliott W. Eisner, "Do American Schools Need Standards?," *The School Administrator,* vol. 51 (May 1994), p. 8–15.

16. C. S. Lewis, *The Abolition of Man* (Macmillan, 1947), p. 35.

17. "Family Income Backgrounds Continue to Determine Chances for Baccalaureate Degree in 1992," *Postsecondary Education Opportunity* (September 1993).

18. David K. Cohen and Michael S. Garet, "Reforming Educational Policy with Applied Social Research," *Harvard Educational Review,* vol. 45 (February 1975), pp. 17–43.

19. Theodore R. Sizer, *Horace's School: Redesigning the American High School* (Houghton Mifflin, 1992).

20. Sigmund Koch, "The Nature and Limits of Psychological Knowledge," in Sigmund Koch and D. E. Leary, eds., *A Century of Psychology as Science* (Washington: American Psychological Association, 1992).

Standards for Education

American schools are underachieving institutions. Their aspirations are too low, and they are not working up to capacity. It is not that students are learning less than before; test scores of basic skills have risen since the mid-1970s. Students are not learning the skills and acquiring the knowledge they will need in the future. Schooling of today was designed early in the twentieth century. The aim was to educate a small elite of future leaders—managers, engineers, physicians, lawyers, and other professionals—to use their minds well. For the others—for most students—educational aims were much more modest. The goal was to teach basic citizenship and to inculcate the limited skills young people would need to take their places as workers in an economy that demanded many more willing hands than active minds. It was a mass production form of education suited to the mass production economy of the time. Broad, liberating education for the many was considered unnecessary and unachievable.

The strategy seemed to work for many decades; living standards rose for more and more Americans, and American democracy seemed secure. But at the beginning of the twenty-first century, the world will have few rewards for individuals or nations that limit themselves to educating only a few to think.[1] To maintain a high-wage economy, almost all individuals will have to think their way through their workdays: analyzing problems, proposing solutions, troubleshooting and repairing equipment, communicating with others, and managing resources of time and materials. For the first time since the Industrial Revolution, the human resource needs of a vibrant economy and the civic requirements of a truly participatory democracy are converging. The time has come for American schools to set their sights higher, to move from their inherited preoccupation with low-level fact and skill learning to goals of thinking, reasoning, and problem solving for every student.

Doing that will require the most thorough revision of aspiration and practice that any set of institutions has ever known. It will mean setting new standards of quality and mobilizing all resources to make sure that every single child—with no exceptions based on race, language of origin, or presumed native ability—has the learning opportunities needed to meet those standards. It will mean reeducating teachers to work in new ways and giving them the authority they will need to set a new course with their students.

Achieving this will require interlocking and coherent changes in several components of the education system, including curriculum, textbooks, teacher preparation, and continuing professional development. For these elements to sustain themselves, fundamental changes also will be needed in school management and in how schools relate to families, communities, and the social service delivery system. Provoking and enabling these interlocking changes constitutes a systemic reform policy, the only kind of policy likely to produce the effects on student achievement that are the object of so much rhetorical and political passion.

PERFORMANCE STANDARDS AND SYSTEMIC CHANGE

Thinking about systemic change requires attending not only to how the elements of a system function together in equilibrium, but also to how they might influence one another in a period of disequilibrium and to which elements might be most susceptible to organized, intentional modification. In most countries, an effort at national improvement of education would begin with attention to curriculum and, perhaps, to organizational structure, including teacher certification requirements. Both of these would fall under the purview of a ministry of education with the power—after consultation appropriate to the country's processes—to impose the curriculum and the new forms of organization. In due course, textbooks, exams, and the content of teacher education programs would change in response to the mandated curriculum.

In countries that have traditions, as the United States, of local instead of national control of education, this approach to changing the system is not available. Some countries, notably Britain, have responded by overthrowing significant aspects of the local control tradition and moving toward a national curriculum. The United States is trying to induce systemic changes without federalizing education and without creating a controlling national curriculum. A different point of departure is needed. What are the possibilities?

Some argue for changes in textbooks, because they serve as a kind of de facto national curriculum. But the market incentives operating on textbook publishers mean that, to change texts, a radical change in demand from purchasers (that is, educators) must first be made. In the American system, textbook publishers are an unlikely engine for new policy or practice.

Others argue that the focus should be on teacher education, because only a very differently prepared teaching force will be able to educate students in the new, more demanding ways that are required for the future. The argument from need is compelling. But for the most part, teacher education is in the hands of institutions with even greater traditions of "local" control than the public schools. Individual faculty at colleges and universities substantially control their own programs of instruction, and no one has proposed a convincing and—at least for the moment—politically viable means of directly inducing the hundreds of institutions responsible for educating teachers to make radical changes in what they do themselves or what they demand of future teachers. Furthermore, even with major changes in preservice teacher education, changing schooling practice would take a long time. Newcomers to any profession are not well positioned to take the lead in changing practice, and for many years to come, the vast majority of teachers will have been educated in the old ways.

Some have proposed beginning with the management structure of education, giving local educators and parents more direct decision-making power. Little doubt seems to exist that such changes are essential to overall systemic reform. Most observers of the school restructuring movement, however, seem to agree that, apart from a few schools with substantial outside resources, experiments in site-based management have rarely been able to produce significant changes in curriculum, teaching, and learning. Perhaps more important, without a change in the surrounding system, individual schools that manage to achieve excellence on their own terms will be fragile, likely to be driven back to ordinary ways of proceeding as soon as they become too visibly successful or their special advocates move on to new challenges.

WHY STANDARDS MATTER

Standards and accompanying assessments thus become a possible point of departure for systemic change. If agreement can be reached on standards for student achievement, and if conditions can be created in schools and school systems all over the country in which those standards are internalized and made the centerpiece of educators' and students' efforts, a good probability exists that curriculum, professional development, textbooks, and, eventually, teacher preparation can be changed so that the entire system is working toward the standards.

The New Standards Project was started in 1990 with this goal in mind.[2] New Standards is a consortium of states and major school districts that have joined together to produce a system of examinations and assessments based on a shared set of high achievement standards. Standards and assessments were to be aimed at what had come to be called the thinking curriculum, an instructional program that would teach children to use knowledge to reason and solve problems and that would carry them well beyond the "basics" that are the staple of American schooling.[3] What is more, this kind of education would be promoted for all children and, if successful, would constitute a veritable revolution in the education system.

Making this kind of transformation in education will require overturning a widely held belief that what people can learn in school depends mainly on their largely inborn aptitude for learning. American schools convey in multiple, often subtle, ways a message that aptitude matters and effort does not. Standardized tests (ranging from the achievement tests used in elementary schools to the Scholastic Aptitude Test) compare students with each other, not with a standard of achievement. Year after year, students take tests that tell them whether they are in a high, average, or low part of the distribution. This system of testing has no way to show the result of academic effort. One can learn, even learn a lot, and still remain in the below-average group. Children who start out low know, however implicitly, that their relative rank is unlikely to change much, unless the high starters were to give up schooling and study for a year. A greater disincentive for work is hard to imagine. And little more incentive exists for the high scorers. Because they are being compared with others, not with a challenging standard, they see little need to study hard.

New Standards aims to change this state of affairs, to replace tests that compare students with each other with exams and portfolio assessments in which they are judged against a known standard of achievement, a standard toward which they can work systematically and cumulatively. This standard will be the same for all students, but some may need extra resources of time and instruction to meet it. An honors standard will ensure that those for whom academic learning is easy will always have a challenge. New Standards partners are committed to a social compact that promises that appropriate instruction and related resources will be made available to all children so that all can honestly aspire to meet the standard. The whole system is to be organized around effort instead of aptitude.

STATUS OF THE STANDARDS MOVEMENT

When the standards revolution began in the late 1980s, many who were involved believed that the process of setting standards would be a straightforward matter. The expectations were that tough decisions would have to be made and that people would disagree about many details of what American students ought to know and be able to do, but that assembling people with a stake and with expertise in each of the disciplines of the school curriculum and, through a process of discussion and consultation, to arrive at a workable consensus would not be difficult. The results of such a process were available in the *Curriculum and Evaluation Standards for School Mathematics, K-12,* which had been crafted under the leadership of the National Council of Teachers of Mathematics (NCTM).[4] These standards were, at the time, being officially and unofficially adopted by states and school districts across the country. Textbook companies announced that their newest editions conformed to the NCTM standards; major testing programs, including the National Assessment of Educational Progress (NAEP), tried to reconfigure their instruments to conform to the NCTM standards. Everything seemed to be in place for a forward-looking, energetic conversion of mathematics education to a set of national standards that were not federally mandated and did not specify a national curriculum. Assuming that other education disciplines could do much the same thing, participants in the standards revolution thought all that was needed was to stimulate and support the process.

That is the origin of the several Department of Education grants to professional associations and other organizations to develop standards.

The process has not gone smoothly. Several years after the initial grants were made for developing standards in English, history, science, and geography, educators and—more important—the public at large are not sure what standards are, and doubts are arising about whether they are needed or wanted. Science and English language arts standard-setting processes are behind schedule and embroiled in conflict. History and geography standards have been written, but controversy exists over whether these two disciplines—in some sense, a revival of an older tradition and, thus, a conservative educational move—can or should occupy all of the terrain and time traditionally devoted to the "social studies." The Goals 2000 legislation, bipartisan in origin and representing a complex political negotiation among two administrations and Congresses and a shifting cohort of state governors, created the National Education Standards and Improvement Council (NESIC), which will review standards submitted by multiple groups (states, districts, and even schools) but has no power to declare any of them the national standards. In Washington, it sometimes appears that political realities have eroded the vision of a nation that is pulling in the same direction, with national education standards that set common aspirations and recruit loyalties of professionals and other people throughout the land.

In many localities, furthermore, the vision is even more tarnished. Communities everywhere, sometimes mobilized by political forces whose interests in education may be secondary to more general political aspirations, are expressing doubts about the whole idea of standards-based systemic education reform. These groups fear that the changes associated with standards and outcomes are more concerned with promoting social values than academic achievement, that outcome-based education—which is hard for many to distinguish from the performance-driven system promoted by the standards community—will dumb down the curriculum and substitute an "anything goes," "feel good" set of values for the tough-minded basics they think the existing curriculum and tests offer. These public doubts are fed by various voices from the professional education community. Some claim that standards coming from anywhere other than an individual school, its students and parents, and its immediately surrounding community are an intrusion on the right of local communities to decide what their schools should teach. Others continue to defend traditional forms of testing against the demands for more authentic assessments that most promoters of standards or performance-based education often advocate.

What is going on? Has the will or the way been lost? Is the standards movement dying and with it the hope of educational achievement at new levels and of new kinds? Or are the confusion and controversy part of a healthy, if painful, birthing process? Perhaps reform-minded educators are witnesses to—and participants in—the creation of a brand new child, an individual whose grown personality is only dimly perceptible now. Controversy and malaise stem in great part from the creation of something new. No working model exists, no technology or political process of educational standard setting that can be borrowed with small adaptations from other countries and then applied in the United States. The NCTM process that seemed so straightforward has turned out to be incomplete. America has been trying to create standards without knowing what an educational standard is. Proponents have been advocating an image of a standards-based system that is inadequately described and for which, as yet, no good examples are available. Critics are reacting to their own image of what education standards might be, and they do not like what they imagine.

EDUCATION STANDARDS AROUND THE WORLD

When the standards movement in education began, many sensible people said, "Let's benchmark. Let's look at what standards are in other countries around the world and then make sure that we do at least as well. We do not need or want to copy other countries. We will want to create our own standards, but we surely need to know what others are doing." The New Standards Project took this suggestion—transformed into a mandate for international benchmarking by its Governing Board—seriously. A relatively simple mission was set: Ask appropriate people in several countries what they expected their students to know and be able to do at key transition points in their educational careers. Some answers were surprising.

First, the new American idea of standards, clear thresholds that nearly all people in the society would be expected to meet, was a puzzlement to most of the informants. They did not know what was meant by the term *standards*. When asked what they expected of students in their elementary and secondary schools, most informants gave answers that involved their national or state curricula. Some also pointed to their nonstatutory guidelines, much more detailed advice to teachers about accepted and effective ways of teaching the curriculum. When we asked how much of what was outlined in the curriculum or specified in the guidelines they actually expected all of their students to learn, the informants said, often ruefully, that was a different matter. Perhaps, they suggested, what needed to be reviewed was their examinations.

Exams, de facto, determine what teachers and students spend time on and so would offer a very practical way of knowing what would be expected, at least for students at the ages at which exams are given. That was very helpful, a much more concrete approach to determining what students were expected to learn. But the expectations for a population cannot be determined until information is provided about who takes which exams, how many pass, and what counts as passing (for example, what kinds of responses to the questions, how many points). So questions were asked about those matters. While deep into the details of the various countries' examination systems, an answer was still being sought to the no longer simple question: "What are your education standards?"

In no country are education standards laid out in a single document that could be carried home and confidently used to communicate with American colleagues. Despite the complexities, the New Standards Governing Board was provided with good information on what is expected of and achieved by students in other countries.[5] This was done by piecing together an account of expectations and achievements in other countries through the answers to four questions: (1) What are students in other countries expected to know and be able to do at key transition points in their schooling careers? (2) What kinds of performances are used to demonstrate competence? (3) What counts as "good enough" in these performances? and (4) What portion of the cohort is meeting the standard?

To determine expectations for what students are expected to know and be able to do in mathematics, language arts, science, and other subject areas, an examination must be made of national or regional curricula as well as textbooks, course syllabi, and, when possible, class work. To learn what kinds of performances are used to demonstrate competence, exams should be collected and analyzed for the relationship of questions on the exams to textbooks and formal curriculum statements. The easiest to find and evaluate are the national or state exams, including information on when they are given and for what purpose. Other groups in the United States have been doing similar work, and extremely helpful reports are now available on the structure and content of high school leaving examinations in several countries.[6] But few countries today give these formal examinations to students before the age of sixteen or so. Therefore, a full picture of the kinds of performances expected in other countries demands that examples be collected of internal school or classroom exams and other evaluation activities.

Even with exams or other assessments in hand, determining what the standards are, however, is not possible until the grading criteria are spelled out—what counts as "good enough" work on the exams or other assessments. So a full standards-detection effort should include a collection of benchmark examples of student work (probably graded exam papers and classwork), along with grading rubrics or guidelines, and, extremely important, teacher commentary on what the scores mean and why the papers have received particular grades. Without this commentary, the standard remains unknown. Finally, knowing what gets a passing or honors grade does not reveal what the real expectations are in a country; also needed to be known is how many students try to pass a particular exam and what proportion succeeds. An exam taken by 30 percent of a country's young people and passed by half of those who try sets a very different kind of standard from one that 80 percent of young people take and that 75 percent are able to pass. Only by comparing equivalent population groups can an understanding of standards be reached. For this purpose, information is collected on pass/fail rates for national exams or, when such data are not available, professional estimates of percentages of students meeting the standards. Data also are gathered on percentages of students proceeding through various schooling streams, so that it can be determined who is taking which exams.

From this research, focused thus far on mathematics, the New Standards Project has learned that countries vary noticeably in the kinds of mathematics they teach, but that, overall, expectations and achievement are considerably higher in many countries than in the

United States. Perhaps the most important early lesson, however, has been the need to rethink what an education standard is.

WHAT IS AN EDUCATIONAL STANDARD?

The complexities encountered in international benchmarking have prompted a reexamination of the original view of how educational standards are established and of what standards are. The conversations held abroad clearly indicated that national education standard setting for the United States will not be accomplished just by commissioning some group, even a properly representative one, to write standards. Such a group could develop statements of what students should know and be able to do, the terms in which the question "What is a standard?" was answered in the past. But such statements by themselves cannot function as standards in the sense intended by those who began actively pressing for a standards-based education system several years ago. What they had in mind was a system in which education achievement would rise because everyone in the system was working toward the same ends and everyone clearly understood what those ends were. Functional standards were needed, standards that could help educators and students understand what to work toward, implemented in a way that would make them desired goals, not bureaucratic impositions. Functional education standards require five components: content statements, performance descriptions, "good enough" criteria, benchmark examples of student work, and commentary on the benchmarks.

Content statements are the starting point. They are what most people think of when they say that groups of people should get together and agree on standards. Content statements come in many flavors, and the labels used—ranging from national curriculum to valued outcomes and from curriculum framework to common core—hardly correlate with the level of detail and specificity of the statements. The Norwegian National Curriculum, for example, devotes ten pages to the curriculum for all grades of compulsory schooling (roughly ages seven to sixteen), providing lists of mathematical topics that are to be covered in three broad age/grade bands (see figure 4). Norway considers its national curriculum "bare bones" in degree of specification and is explicitly concerned with maintaining room for local options in

FIGURE 4. *Excerpts from the Norwegian National Curriculum Guidelines for Mathematics*

MAIN AREAS OF STUDY AND TOPICS

- Problem Solving
- Number
- Numerical Calculation
- Measurement and Units of Measurement
- Percentage
- Statistics
- Personal Economy and National Economy
- Algebra and the Theory of Functions
- Computer Studies

NUMBER

Well-founded concepts of number form the basis for all further instruction in Mathematics. For this reason it is necessary, throughout the compulsory school, to do thorough work to develop clear concepts of number and a clear understanding of number.

The pupils must learn to see the connection between quantities and numerals (symbols of number) and between the order and size of numbers. In addition, they must work on the terms and symbols used when comparing numbers of different magnitude. The pupils must receive a thorough introduction to the decimal system.

In the first year in particular, special emphasis should be placed on work using concrete materials.

The number axis can be used as an illustration in the introduction to fractions, decimals and positive and negative numbers.

Grades 1-3

Understanding and handling of numbers, limited to positive integers and zero: Numbers connected to quantity, order of numbers, the expressions equal to, larger/more than, smaller/less than.

The decimal system: Special emphasis on using the numbers 0-1000.

Fractions: Examples of the most common fractions, such as a half, a third, a quarter.

Grades 4-6

Even numbers, odd numbers, prime numbers, composite numbers: Introduction to the concepts.

Decimal system: Extension of the number series, with special emphasis on numbers up to one million.

Fractions: Making fractions, improper fractions, mixed numbers, equal fractions.

Decimals: Relation between fractions and decimals, especially $0.1 = 1/10$ and $0.01 = 1/100$. Order of numbers.

Positive and negative numbers: Positive and negative numbers in specific connections.

Grades 7-9

Even numbers, odd numbers, prime numbers, composite numbers.

Fractions: Fractions as ratios.

Decimals: Order of numbers. Decimal places. Relation between fractions and decimals.

Rounding off and approximation: Evaluation of number of decimals.

Indices: Main emphasis on powers of ten. Squares and square roots.

Overview of number fields: Positive integers, whole numbers, rational numbers, real numbers.

Source: Ministry of Education and Research, *Curriculum Guidelines for Compulsory Education in Norway* (W. Nygaard, Norway: H. Aschehong and Co., 1987), pp. 213–14.

education. The national curriculum in France—a country famed for its centralized, Napoleonic school system—specifies the topics in more detail than does Norway's curriculum (the math program for the five years of primary school occupies thirteen pages of text). But, as in Norway, little specification of pedagogy is offered (see figure 5). The Norwegian and French national curricula typify what was found in European countries and in Japan: some broad philosophical statements, followed by lists of topics. Of the six components of standard setting, only the first, content statements, can be found in these national curricula.

In the United States, the term *national curriculum* is taboo. But most states have developed curriculum guidelines to loosely govern their public schools. The state documents are, with a few exceptions (for example, the California *Curriculum Frameworks*), mostly statements of broad goals. Like the European national curricula, they are limited to content statements that are too general to provide real guidance to schools or parents. For example, among the fifty-three outcomes specified by the Pennsylvania State Board of Education are seven mathematics content statements covering kindergarten through high school (see figure 6). Wide agreement exists that statements such as Pennsylvania's, which are similar in level of specificity and in language to those of many other states, are not specific enough to serve as functional guidelines for teaching and learning. In some states, work is under way to develop more specific statements that will apply across the state. In others, including Pennsylvania, each school district is expected to take steps to translate goal or outcome statements into content standards that they think all students should meet. All over the United States, committees of teachers, sometimes with parents and community members, are struggling with a task for which they have little support. They turn, when they can, to the standards documents of the professional associations, the National Council of Teachers of Mathematics, and the others that were funded by the federal government. Can they find help there in developing performance descriptions, good enough criteria, or any of the other elements of a functional standards system? Only in part.

Content statements are a start at specifying education standards, but knowing what they mean is difficult without some further statements describing how one could decide whether a student had mastered the content. Such statements are performance descriptions,

FIGURE 5. *French National Curriculum: Mathematics for Grades 4-5 (8eme-7eme)*

MATHEMATICS FOR THE *COURS MOYEN*

The student continues to study and increases his understanding of whole numbers and the four operations, begins to work with decimals and fractions, tackles proportionality, improves his knowledge of geometric objects, refines his tracing and constructions skills, and carries out measurements.

A. Arithmetic
- Writing, naming and comparing whole numbers. Introduction of decimals and simple fractions.
- Writing and naming decimals.
- Determining a decimal by addition, subtraction, multiplication and division; translating fractions into decimals.
- Comparing decimals.
- Problems involving addition, subtraction, multiplication and division; developing the ability to manipulate decimals with the four operations, both mental and written, as well as with a pocket calculator.
- Recognition and use of numerical functions: n Æ n+a and n Æ n x a, and their reciprocals, defined for all decimals. Work with problems relevant to these functions and especially to proportionality (e.g. the rule of 3).
- Application of the procedures of mental calculation for decimals, using the four operations and the numerical functions already studied.

B. Geometry
- Reproduction, description representation and construction of various geometric objects (solids, surfaces, lines).
- Applying transformations to these geometric objects (translation, rotation, symmetry).
- using tools: pencil and paper, centimeter paper, ruler, T-square, compass, templates.
- employing techniques of reproduction and construction: transfer of distances; reproduction, enlargement or reduction of a design made out of squares; drawing parallel and perpendicular lines.
- Using a logically articulated syntax and the vocabulary of geometry: cube, edge, height, face, sphere, triangle, quadrilateral, parallelogram, rectangle, trapezoid, square, side, diagonal, circle, disc.

C. Measurement of certain magnitudes
- Formation of the concepts of length, area, volume, mass, angle and duration; using systems of measurement; expressing, with numbers or tables, the results of an exercise in measuring.
- Using the units of the legal and conventional systems of measurement.
- Calculating with numbers expressed as measurements of length or weight.
- Measuring the perimeter of a circle, the area of a disc, the area of a rectangle, the area of a triangle, the volume of a prism.
- Using a formula to calculate the area or the volume of a given object.

Source: Ministere de l'education nationale de la jeunesse et des sports direction des ecoles, *Les cycles a l'ecole primaire* [The program of study for primary schools], trans. Katherine J. Nolan (Paris: Centre national de documentation pedagogique, 1991).

FIGURE 6. *Mathematics Outcomes in Pennsylvania*

MATHEMATICS

(i) All students use numbers, number systems and equivalent forms (including numbers, words, objects and graphics) to represent theoretical and practical situations.

(ii) All students compute, measure and estimate to solve theoretical and practical problems, using appropriate tools, including modern technology such as calculators and computers.

(iii) All students apply the concepts of patterns, functions and relations to solve theoretical and practical problems.

(iv) All students formulate and solve problems and communicate the mathematical processes used and the reasons for using them.

(v) All students understand and apply basic concepts of algebra, geometry, probability and statistics to solve theoretical and practical problems.

(vi) All students evaluate, infer and draw appropriate conclusions from charts, tables and graphs, showing the relationships between data and real-world situations.

(vii) All students make decisions and predictions based upon the collection, organization, analysis and interpretation of statistical data and the application of probability.

Source: Pennsylvania State Board of Education Curriculum, *Pennsylvania Bulletin*, vol. 23, no. 3 (1993), title 22, chapter 5.

statements of what a student might do to demonstrate knowledge or skill. The flagship standards document, produced by the NCTM, takes some steps in this direction. This 258-page document lays out standards for kindergarten through twelfth-grade mathematics. It explicitly embraces a new body of content and a new pedagogy for mathematics, with more focus on conceptual understanding, problem solving, and communication in mathematics and less on the traditional practice of computation. The standards for primary school (K-4) occupy fifty-eight pages. This is more than four times as long as the French national curriculum in math for those ages. Its level of detail in content statements is close to that of the Norwegian curriculum (see figure 7). Numerous examples of teaching activity and of student work fill the many pages of the NCTM document (see figure 8). These

FIGURE 7. *Overview of the National Council of Teachers of Mathematics Standard for K-4 and Detail of Standard 5 (Estimation), Grades K-4*

CURRICULUM STANDARDS FOR GRADES K-4 OVERVIEW

1. Mathematics as Problem Solving
2. Mathematics as Communication
3. Mathematics as Reasoning
4. Mathematical Connections
5. Estimation
6. Number Sense and Numeration
7. Concepts of Whole Number Operations
8. Whole Number Computation
9. Geometry and Spatial Sense
10. Measurement
11. Statistics and Probability
12. Fractions and Decimals
13. Patterns and Relationships

STANDARD 5: ESTIMATION

In grades K-4, the curriculum should include estimation so students can –
- explore estimation strategies
- recognize when an estimate is appropriate
- apply estimation in working with quantities, measurement, computation, and problem solving

---

Source: National Council of Teachers of Mathematics, *Curriculum and Evaluation Standards for School Mathematics, K-12* (Reston, Va., 1989), pp. 15, 36.

examples are the first performance descriptions to appear in a standards document, although the term *performance standards* had not yet been promulgated when NCTM published its standards. The examples given are illustrative instead of systematic. Not all content statements are accompanied by performance descriptions, and no claim is made that the student work shown constitutes benchmark work, for no criteria of acceptable (good enough) performance are offered. Nevertheless, the NCTM standards comes closer to offering functional standards than any of the European documents.

The NCTM standards are the best approximation of functional standards, but they are only a first approximation. Without systematic illustration and carefully described criteria for what constitutes a good enough performance, an almost good enough one, and an honors one, teachers, students, and parents cannot know what they should be aiming for. Good enough criteria are, in effect, standards for grading pieces of student work, scoring rubrics in the language of performance assessment specialists. Without these judging criteria, standards for performance have not been formulated, because verbal performance descriptions alone cannot create agreement about what is a good enough piece of work.

Extensive experience in grading essay examinations, both in the United States and abroad, clearly indicates that even well-polished statements of grading criteria do not adequately convey a performance standard. Benchmark examples of student work, with commentary, are needed. Examples are used to teach difficult concepts, especially those with fuzzy boundaries. Definitions and rules are used to guide in examining cases, but careful analysis and comparison of cases build the capacity to make judgments about quality. Education standards require quality judgments about student performances. And so, the setting and spreading of education standards will require examples of student work, along with the commentary that helps teachers, parents, and students themselves learn to make quality judgments. Wherever examinations are used in establishing and maintaining educational standards—and that is in most of the world—some system for selecting benchmark papers is used to ensure that graders are all applying the same quality criteria to the papers they evaluate. The benchmark papers are selected by individuals or by groups of teachers. Those who do the selecting are always required to defend their choices, that is, to be able to say why they assigned the grades they did and how each paper succeeds or fails based on the agreed-on quality criteria.

In countries with a long history of examinations, exam papers from past years can provide the examples of different levels of work that people need to make standards functional. In countries in which standards have not been publicly set before and in which no examination tradition exists to draw upon, benchmark work needs to be provided as part of the formal standards documentation. Australia—a country that, like the United States, has only recently attempted to set national education standards—has the best developed example of using benchmark pieces of work with commentary to communicate education standards. The Australian *Curriculum Profile* combines statements of

FIGURE 8. *Performance Description of National Council of Teachers of Mathematics Standard 3 (Mathematics as Reasoning), Grades 5–8*

If given opportunities to reason from graphs about interesting situations, students can develop an appreciation for the problem-solving potential of making, using, and talking about graphs. The following example (Swan 1985) offers a flavor of the potential of graphical representations as tools for reasoning.

Students are given a carefully drawn picture of a roller-coaster track (fig. 3.2).

Fig. 3.2. Roller coaster

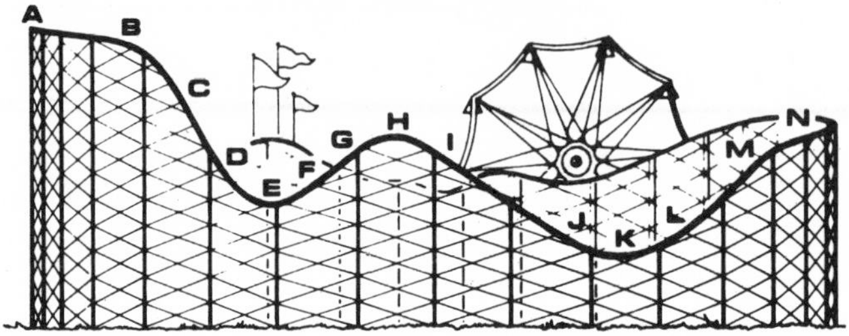

The challenge is to sketch a graph (with no numbers) to represent the speed of the roller coaster versus its position on the track.

Now, to reverse the problem, students are given a part of the graph of speed versus position for another roller coaster (fig. 3.3). The question becomes,

good enough criteria with benchmark student work and explanatory commentary (see figure 9).

Nothing of the range and quality of the Australian profiles is available in the United States. Furthermore, none of the national standards groups has announced its intention to develop education standards in this systematic way. To fill the gap, the New Standards Project will develop a set of performance standards for each of the subject matters in which it is currently working: English language arts, science, mathematics, and applied learning. These standards, which will be ready for public review and commentary in the summer of 1995, will include, for each subject, a set of content statements, performance descriptions, grading criteria, and benchmark examples with commentary. The examples will be drawn in large part from the student work that is being produced in hundreds of classrooms around the country that are participating in New Standards examinations and New Standards portfolio tryouts. The participation of hundreds of

What does the roller-coaster track look like?

Investigating graphical representations and their relationships to algebraic representations can give students a real sense of the dynamic rela tionship between the variables. Such problem settings also allow students to reason directly to, and hypothetically from, graphs.

Students can develop their spatial reasoning abilities in a variety of inter esting settings. They can gather a collection of small objects, such as spools, golf balls, small footballs, small cans and bottles, and foam cups, and then try to draw what they think the shape of the shadow of each object might look like. Students can then test their conjectures by using the overhead projector to cast shadows; they can also be asked to identify the object solely on the appearance of its shadow. Relating the size of the shadow to the size of the object also allows the use of proportional thinking.

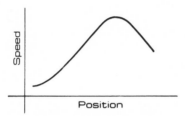

Fig. 3.3 Roller-coaster graph

Source: National Council of Teachers of Mathematics, *Curriculum and Evaluation Standards for School Mathematics, K-12* (Reston, Va., 1989), p. 83.

teachers and thousands of students in the standards development process is part of a strategy for making education standards the linchpin of a reform strategy aimed at improving achievement, not just measuring it. For the strategy to work, one more crucial component must be considered: giving the standards away, making them the intellectual property of students and teachers everywhere.

INTERNALIZED STANDARDS

When education standards were first promoted as a key element of education reform, many people viewed them as a step toward a national test to be imposed on students throughout the nation. Some liked that idea; others feared it. Our judgment was that a national test

FIGURE 9. *Benchmark Student Work with Commentary*

Life and Living

Level 3
WORK SAMPLE

Task

Draw in and label as many body parts and body systems as possible on a body outline, giving reasons for your decisions.

Background

The task was set for seven primary students to find out what they could recall about the parts of the human body. The class first discussed the relative size and position of some major organs and their functions within a number of systems and then worked in separate groups of boys and girls. The original drawings used colour to signify function and relationship.

Relevant outcomes

Life and living

3.8 Identifies external and internal features of living things that work together to form systems with particular functions.

Working scientifically

3.13 Suggests ways of doing investigations, giving consideration to fairness.

3.14 Organises and uses equipment to gather and present information.

3.15 Argues conclusions on the basis of collected information and personal experience.

Summary comment

The students are working at level 3.

THIS IS KELLY M

Our group each made a list of body words then we joined as pairs and then we made a group of 4. We traced Kelly Ms body and then we had a meeting about each part of the body. We had to decide on the shape, place, colour and size. So we startted with the heart. Kelly did the bones, Becky did the heart, lungs and blood. Hollie did the face and sex parts and I did the rest. We don't know how the bones are joined and didn't know how to show nerves. **A**

Heart which pumps to keep us alive. It takes blood to the hands and feet and the brain. It brings blood back from there. **D**

2 lungs which have spaghetti things inside to make us breath. **D**

Stomach which holds all the food. It gets big and expands when you eat too much. **D**

Bladder – we think it is round and gets bigger when you want to go to the toilet. **D**

Questions we want to find out about.

1. How are our bones joined up?

2. What makes us blink?

3. How long is the intestine?

4. What are ther bones called?

5. Where are the nerves?

6. What do the lungs look like if you get astma?

7. What does the appendix do?

8. What makes the breasts grow?

9. What are the sausage intestine things called?

10. Why do you get pimples?

B

(3.13) Develops alternative strategies for doing investigations (**A**); focus questions devised individually and in groups to assist planning (**B**).

(3.14) Diagram chosen to clearly and logically present group findings (**C**).

(3.15) Proposes possible conclusions on basis of experiences and understandings (**D**).

(3.8) Coloured blood vessels (red and blue) indicate an understanding of an interrelated body system (**E**); the placement of body parts demonstrates a good understanding of the position of body parts and some systems (**F**).

Science profile

Source: Curriculum Corporation, *Science—A Curriculum Profile for Australian Schools* (Carlton, Australia, 1994), p. 53.

would make little difference in achievement, which is the real goal of the standards effort. Standards documents, even elegant ones with benchmarks and commentary, can affect achievement only if the standards come to be held as personal goals by teachers and students. For that to happen, teachers and students need to be thinking about, talking about, and guiding their work toward standards every day. That will happen only if a concerted effort is made to engage teachers and students in a massive and continuing conversation about what students should learn, what kinds of work they should do, and how well they should be expected to do it. That is what the New Standards system is designed to promote. There are two parts to the process: grading performance examinations and developing portfolios.

Learning to grade performances according to scoring rubrics that express agreed-on good enough criteria is a powerful introduction to the idea and practice of standards-based education. New Standards in the fall of 1994 would conduct its first partnerwide reference examination in mathematics. Fifth- and eighth-grade students in a sample of schools across the country would spend two class periods answering open-ended questions that engage them in using mathematics concepts and skills to solve relatively complex problems. Some of the problems would take a full class period to answer; others, five or ten minutes. For most problems, students must justify their answers in writing, and the quality of their justifications, as well as the mathematical correctness of the answers, determines the score they will get (see figure 10).

Preparing for the official reference examination and setting the grading standards for it required two years to develop procedures that would yield reliable grading of students' responses—that is, grades that were fair—because several different judges would assign the same grade to a piece of work. The process that has worked is very similar to the one used in grading official school leaving examinations in European countries. A set of benchmark papers was selected for each grade and then trainee scorers—all teachers—were engaged in a process of attempting to predict the benchmark grade.[7] They do this, under the guidance of a trained leader (also a teacher), by discussing each paper at length, comparing its features with the criteria laid out in the scoring rubrics, and defending their judgments to one another. The discussions have the character of an intensive intellectual seminar on the qualities of student work, but after several hours, they lead to a

FIGURE 10. *A New Standards Performance Task for Grade 8*

How Long Should a Shoelace Be?

Suppose you work for a shoelace company. You receive the following assignment from your boss.

 **Sports Laces**

ASSIGNMENT

We have decided to sell laces for sports shoes. We will sell different lengths for shoes with different numbers of eyelets. We will offer lengths for sport shoes that have 4 eyelets all the way up to 18 eyelets (no odd numbers, of course). No one has ever sold so many different lengths for sports shoes before. You have to figure out what lengths to make and which lengths go with which shoes, based on the number of eyelets.

We collected some data from store customers last week. It is confusing because there haven't been very many lengths available. That means that sometimes the customers have had to use lengths that are too short or too long. That's not what we want! We want a unique length for each number of eyelets.

DATA FROM STORE CUSTOMERS WITH SPORTS SHOES

Customer I.D.	Lace Length (inches)	Eyelets (numbers)	Customer I.D.	Lace Length (inches)	Eyelets (numbers)
A	45	8	G	54	12
B	54	10	H	24	4
C	26	4	I	72	14
D	63	14	J	54	12
E	63	12	K	72	16
F	36	8	L	72	18

Write your decisions about lace length so the advertising people making the sign can understand it. They want a table, so customers can look up the number of eyelets and find out the length of lace. They also want a rule, so customers who don't like tables can use the rule to figure out the lengths. Don't worry about making it pretty, they will do that, just make sure the mathematics is right. You better explain how your decisions make sense, so the advertising people will understand.

Thanks.

YOUR BOSS,

Angela

Write a response to your boss Angela's assignment:

- A table that shows for each number of eyelets (even numbers only) how long you have decided the laces should be

- A rule that a customer can use to figure out the length based on the number of eyelets. Don't forget the bow. If you can, express your rule as a formula.

- An explanation of your decisions (tell why they make sense).

remarkable convergence of judgments. Scorers must meet a criterion of matching the benchmark grade on sixteen of twenty papers. Almost all participants reported that the training experience was among the most important professional opportunities in their careers and that they are coming to understand what kinds of work they ought to be asking of their own students and what kinds of quality expectations they should be establishing in their own classrooms. In other words, the process yields reliable grades, but it does far more than that: It makes the standards the intellectual property of the teachers. This is step one in giving standards away.

The next step is to give the standards away to students, to make the expectations and the grading criteria clear to them, and to invite them to gear their efforts to meeting the standards. The major vehicle for this is the *Student Portfolio Handbook*. Portfolios of student work, collected over several years, culled, corrected, and reworked until the pieces submitted represent the best evidence that each individual can offer that he or she can do what is expected, are the best way to bring standards into everyday practice. If attention is limited to formal examinations, educators would have far less impact on what students do from day to day and on what counts on their transcripts and in their lives, than if the regular work that students do is treated as part of the official grading system. In the fall of 1994, in several hundred schools, New Standards began a field trial of a portfolio system aimed at doing that. Teachers would be critical partners in this trial, as they will be once the portfolio system is running officially. But the most important partners in a system based on grading of students' classwork are the students.

Students were spoken to directly in a set of handbooks outlining the standards to which their work should be directed and suggesting how the portfolio itself should be judged (see figure 11). Every student in a New Standards portfolio field trial class would receive a copy of this handbook. Every classroom would receive a collection of exemplary student work that teachers and students can use to guide them through the initially unfamiliar process of preparing a standards-based portfolio. In future years, scoring rubrics and graded benchmark portfolios will further guide student efforts. When the system is fully functioning, an auditing system on portfolio grades—which will be assigned, in the first instance, by teachers in the students' own school—will further ensure that grades mean the same thing from one school to the next. An audited portfolio grading system (probably

FIGURE 11. *Standard for a Writing Portfolio*

STANDARD 1 IN WRITING:
Technical Competence and Effectiveness
Communicate clearly, effectively and without errors.

Possible evidence to show you met Standard 1 in Writing

One essay with various drafts in which you demonstrate that you corrected errors and revised the essay to make it clearer and more effective • a comparison of the challenges faced by two characters in different novels • a business plan • an essay narrating an event in your life • a detailed response to an article • instructions for organizing a debate • a report on a complex topic.

Getting a piece of writing in shape takes time and a little patience. You have to plan your writing, scratch out a first draft, read what you have so far, reorganize, revise and refine — all the while weeding out flaws like misspelled words and bad grammar. Show us you can:

- *Use correct spelling, mechanics, grammar, usage, paragraph structure and punctuation to make your points.*
- *Explain your ideas clearly.* This means choosing the best word to say what you mean and structuring sentences so that their meaning is clear. Put in the details that will help the reader understand the point you are making. During the revision process, you can ask yourself, "Is my writing clear enough so that readers know what I'm trying to say? How can I make my second draft more effective than my first?"
- *Organize your writing coherently, so that it flows logically.* Whether you've written a report, a story or a letter, the reader should be able to follow what you're trying to say from start to finish. That means paragraphs should link to one another, with transitions connecting one idea to the next.
- *Use a variety of writing strategies.* Choose among the many writing styles and techniques available to you. For example, save the shocking plot twist in your short story until the very end. Use flashbacks; or begin an essay or story with a rhetorical question or a description of a compelling scene or event.
- *Make connections among ideas and interpretations.* Use writing to explore and expand on ideas from literature and real-life issues. That could mean using the books you read in English class (maybe *To Kill a Mockingbird*) to help you write a better essay about life in the American South in your history class. Or it could

anchored by one or two common projects that students in many schools include in their portfolios) will mean that families, colleges, and employers can trust students' grades. The grade of A from an inner-city school will mean the same as an A from an upscale suburban school when both are based on an audited portfolio system. Making standards public and clear and equivalent in this way is part

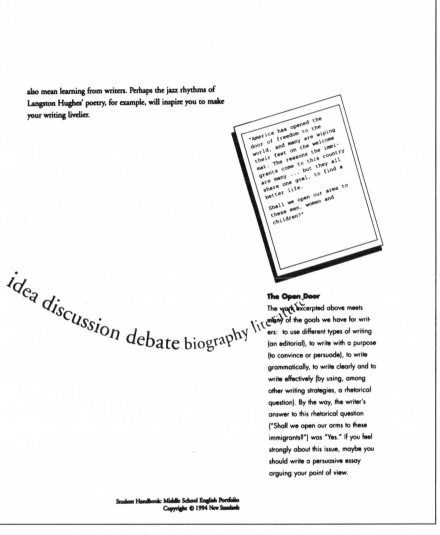

also mean learning from writers. Perhaps the jazz rhythms of
Langston Hughes' poetry, for example, will inspire you to make
your writing livelier.

"America has opened the
door of freedom to the
world, and many are wiping
their feet on the welcome
mat. The reasons the immigrants come to this country
are many ... but they all
share one goal, to find a
better life.
Shall we open our arms to
these men, women and
children?"

idea discussion debate biography literature

The Open Door
The work excerpted above meets
many of the goals we have for writers: to use different types of writing
(an editorial), to write with a purpose
(to convince or persuade), to write
grammatically, to write clearly and to
write effectively (by using, among
other writing strategies, a rhetorical
question). By the way, the writer's
answer to this rhetorical question
("Shall we open our arms to these
immigrants?") was "Yes." If you feel
strongly about this issue, maybe you
should write a persuasive essay
arguing your point of view.

Student Handbook: Middle School English Portfolio
Copyright © 1994 New Standards

Source: New Standards Project, *Student Portfolio Handbook: Middle School Language Arts,*
field trial version (Pittsburgh and Washington, 1994), pp. 12–13.

of the New Standards equity agenda. It will constitute a major step
toward equalizing the opportunities of students from poor and minority families to participate in high-expectation learning activities.

CONCLUSION

How are educators doing at establishing standards for American education? The simple view that many proponents of standards appeared to hold in the heady opening years of the standards movement must be modified. Establishing standards is not, in America's contentious democracy, a simple matter. Making standards functional—so that they do the intended work of raising achievement throughout the land and among all children—will be a long-term prospect. A standards-based education system represents a profound change for America. It should not be surprising that the job is not already done.

Yet the country has made a very good start. In only three years, draft content standards have been created in several disciplines. Many states are moving to create standards frameworks that can provide an important policy tool and foundation for changed education practice. Those working in the field have a much clearer sense of the scope of the task ahead, and there is promise of major progress toward functional performance standards in 1995. Concrete models of functional standards, together with demonstrations of their power to markedly improve learning in a wide cohort of schools, are the best hope for rebuilding confidence in public school and its possibilities.

NOTES

1. Commission on the Skills of the American Workforce, *America's Choice! High Skills or Low Wages* (Rochester, N.Y.: National Center on Education and the Economy, 1990); R. Marshall and M. Tucker, *Thinking for a Living: Education and the Wealth of Nations* (Basic Books, 1992); and R. B. Reich, *The Work of Nations: Preparing Ourselves for Twenty-first Century Capitalism* (Knopf, 1991).

2. Members of the New Standards Project are the states of Arkansas, California, Colorado, Connecticut, Delaware, Iowa, Kentucky, Maine, Massachusetts, Missouri, New York, Oregon, Pennsylvania, Texas, Vermont, and Washington and the cities of Fort Worth, Texas; New York, New York; Pittsburgh, Pennsylvania; Rochester, New York; San Diego, California; and White Plains, New York. Together they enroll about 50 percent of all U.S. public school children. The New Standards Project is a joint undertaking of the Learning Research and Development Center at the University of Pittsburgh and the National Center on Education and the Economy in Rochester, New

York. It is funded by grants from the Pew Charitable Trusts, the John D. and Catherine T. MacArthur Foundation, the U.S. Department of Education, and the dues of the Partners.

3. Lauren B. Resnick and L. E. Klopfer, eds., *Toward the Thinking Curriculum: Current Cognitive Research* (Alexandria, Va.: Association for Supervision and Curriculum Development, 1989).

4. National Council of Teachers of Mathematics, *Curriculum and Evaluation Standards for School Mathematics, K-12* (Reston, Va., 1989).

5. Lauren B. Resnick, Katherine J. Nolan, and D. P. Resnick, "Benchmarking Education Standards," *Education Evaluation and Policy Analysis* (forthcoming); and Katherine J. Nolan, *Mathematics Education in Five Nations*, report to the New Standards Governing Board (University of Pittsburgh, Learning Research and Development Center, 1994).

6. American Federation of Teachers, National Center for Improving Science Education, The Network, *What College-Bound Students Abroad Are Expected to Know about Biology: Defining World Class Standards*, vol. 1 (Washington, 1994); L. V. Cheney, *National Tests: What Other Countries Expect Their Students to Know* (Washington: National Endowment for the Humanities, 1991); and M. A. Eckstein and H. J. Noah, *Secondary School Examinations: International Perspectives on Policies and Practice* (Yale University Press, 1993).

7. New Standards uses a 4-point grading scale, in which 4 counts as "meets the standard" and 4+ counts as honors. Benchmark papers must be created for a 4 (passing) grade, a 3, a 2, a 1, and the honors grade.

Who's Afraid of the Big, Bad Test?

The phrase *national testing* evokes uneasy images that may have their origins in the U.S. experience with college entrance exams. Millions of students sit poised with number two pencils sharpened, dripping with nervousness in thousands of test centers across the land, as stern, sharp-eyed monitors distribute sealed booklets at precisely the same instant. Three hours later, the smudged booklets are dispatched to some distant location where computers process them and then print out numbers that permanently affect the life prospects of the young test-takers.

An arrangement that seems stressful and harsh to seventeen-year-olds who are voluntarily submitting to it can appear practically sadistic, even faintly un–American, when nine-year-olds are put to the test but on a compulsory basis, especially if the federal government is involved.

From the students' standpoint, such an experience would not differ appreciably from situations already familiar in nearly every school in the land, where state and local exams, commercial tests, aptitude tests, achievement tests and many others are regularly administered in much the same manner. That is also one reason that many educators resist adding to the present burden of testing. They tend to recite statements such as "American students are the most heavily tested in the world."

But burdensomeness is only one facet of this complex debate, which also involves profound differences in educational philosophy, arguments about the nature of American federalism, disagreement over what motivates children and adults to strive, disputes over the nature and purpose of testing, differing views about fairness, tension over the place of accountability in education policy, and more than a trace of envy, greed, ego, and partisanship.

Unlike many other complicated disputes, however, this one is important. For if, as seems likely, the United States fails to meet the ambitious end-of-decade national education goals that George Bush and the fifty governors set for it in 1990, a sizable part of the reason will be the refusal to construct any sort of meaningful examination or assessment system tied to those goals. The success that opponents and critics of national testing have had in fending off and delegitimizing this idea almost certainly reduces the "national goals process" to a noble, hollow gesture that will have little effect on people's behavior, hence will produce scant change in what they learn.

Worse, the debate over national testing, the actions taken by Congress to prevent anything like it from coming to pass, and the coincidental but savage backlash against "outcome-based education" may also deter states and localities from creating their own assessment and accountability systems. To the extent that this occurs, the entire reform movement that began with *A Nation at Risk* will be slowed.

WHY TEST?

The word *national* accounts for most of the heat, but the principle of testing is more important—and just as controversial, at least within the education field. In other domains of American life, testing is taken for granted. It is reassuring. Demands may be heard for even more of it, especially if the matter at hand is significant. Who would knowingly fly on a plane that had not been fully and recently tested? Go up with a pilot whose prowess at the controls had never been examined? Dive fifty feet under water in scuba gear whose functioning had not been thoroughly checked with a guide who was not certified? Swallow a medication that the Food and Drug Administration had not vetted? Submit to surgery by a doctor whose knowledge and skills had not been examined and certified? Buy a house that had not passed its termite test? Purchase a gold ring if the jeweler did not verify its 22 carats through an assay? Own stock in a company that has not had its books independently audited?

Tests serve diverse purposes. They help to show if self-interested claims and brash assertions are true. To judge whether someone or something can be trusted to be what it says. To determine a product's value. To determine whether certain standards have been met. (While the standards cannot be described, trust is placed in the standard-setting body and its examination process.) To distinguish services, products, individuals, and institutions from one another in ways that plumb below surface appearances, and to make comparisons and decisions based on those distinctions. To spot problems and diagnose shortcomings, either to pass judgment on them (and, perhaps, cut losses) or to take corrective action before too much time and money are squandered.

Tests are used in small matters of taste, comfort, and convenience. (Is the cake done in the center? Is the milk the right temperature for baby?) They are used for personal safety. (Check the smoke detectors every six months to make sure they are still working. Do not buy a car seat or microwave that got low marks from the Underwriters' Laboratory.) They are used to promote public health and safety. (Residents are advised to boil their drinking water when water quality tests reveal a problem. People are not supposed to drive a car if they have not passed a driver's license test.) And they are used in many different ways in the education system.

Teachers use tests of their own devising to see if particular lessons have had the intended effect and whether individual pupils have learned what they should. Communities and states use tests—their own, or those developed by commercial vendors—to determine whether standards are being met, whether youngsters are ready to graduate from high school, whether teachers and principals deserve bonuses, whether various programs and policies are working as planned, and whether certain schools or school districts need help, intervention, public accolades, or public humiliation. Colleges use them to ascertain whether Sally and Jack are fit candidates for admission, if they have learned enough German to fulfill the language requirement, whether to confer college credit for the Advanced Placement history course, and what section of calculus (or remedial algebra) to place them in.

Scholars and researchers use tests for every imaginable form of inquiry and evaluation (and for some that could be imagined only by members of the American Educational Research Association). Private groups use test scores to decide who gets invited to participate in special summer programs and who receives merit scholarships. Pollsters, newspapers and magazines, and national organizations employ tests to see how well particular subjects are being learned or to buttress their claims and contentions. The federal government uses tests for sundry purposes, including monitoring educational progress, comparing U.S. achievement with that of other countries, evaluating the effectiveness of federal programs, spotting signs of discrimination, studying the effects of various factors in children's lives and school practices, and screening people who want to enlist in the Army.

Behind—seldom far behind—these hundreds of uses of thousands of tests is private enterprise. The U.S. testing industry, an unusual mix of for-profit and nonprofit (but sometimes very wealthy) firms, takes in hundreds of millions of dollars annually by developing and supplying most of these tests and often by administering, scoring, and analyzing their results. It is a fast-growing industry, entangled with giant conglomerates (big publishing firms own most of the commercial test-makers), with high-status education organizations (for example, the College Board), with elaborate relationships (and lobbying) at every level of government, with the reputations of eminent individuals and the benefactions of prominent foundations, and—perhaps especially—with the ways that Americans perceive the performance of their schools and their own children.

It is not unfailingly an admirable industry. Test makers, sellers, and buyers sometimes join to mislead the public. Evidence has accumulated over the years of tests promoted and used because they yield happier results for a particular community or state than do other tests. One notorious result, dubbed the "Lake Wobegon effect," is that nearly all states and communities have been able to report that their students are scoring "above the national average" or "above grade level."[1] The primary point is not that the testing industry misbehaves; it is that no discussion of U.S. testing should proceed very far without recognizing the large financial and reputational interests associated with that industry.

TESTING AND EDUCATION REFORM

In recent years, testing has come to be seen by many as an important element of the "excellence movement," the reform effort intended to change the education system so that U.S. children acquire stronger skills and greater knowledge.

Test results have much to do with the origins of that movement: international comparisons; sagging Scholastic Aptitude Test (SAT) scores; national assessment results that, in most subjects and grade levels, slumped during the 1970s. Academics still debate the causes of test score decline and more than a few educators have rationalized it, but employers, governors, and critics used those downward-sloping lines as evidence that something was amiss and needed fixing.

Not surprisingly, the barometers that indicated the presence of a storm were consulted by those looking to see if the weather was improving. But that is only part of the reason for the emphasis on—and nervousness about—testing.

Testing is also the linchpin in an entire education reform strategy that gained prominence as the 1980s wore on. Simplifying an elaborate tale, many of the reforms undertaken in the early part of that decade had focused on changes in school resources and practices. The assumption was that, if the day were extended, more academic courses taken, more preschool programs offered, class size reduced, research findings more methodically disseminated, teachers better trained (or allowed into the classroom with less formal pedagogical training), textbooks replaced, computers purchased, magnet schools created and choices widened, more governance decisions made at the school level, and so forth and so on, children would learn more.

Arguments still rage as to whether any of these changes helped and whether they were given a fair opportunity to succeed. But no dispute exists that a lot was tried, that a great deal more money was invested in education, and that results were only slightly better at the end of the decade than at the beginning.

Many exasperated reformers accordingly began to focus directly on the results themselves and on an alternative paradigm for change that essentially said: Stop fiddling with school resources, practices, services, and regulations, and, instead, state precisely what results are expected. Free schools and educators to generate those results however they think best. In return for that freedom, hold them accountable for producing—and demonstrating that they have produced—the desired results, not for just going through the motions. Reward individuals and institutions that succeed. Punish, or intervene in, those that fail.

Perhaps the first clear expression of this approach by policymakers, found in the same document that signaled the governors' arrival as a major force in education reform, was a 1986 manifesto from the National Governors' Association (NGA) called *Time for Results.* In its introduction, NGA chairman (as well as Tennessee governor and future U.S. education secretary) Lamar Alexander wrote that "the

Governors are ready for some old-fashioned horse-trading. We'll regulate less, if schools and school districts will produce better results."[2]

This standards and accountability model of education reform made sense to elected officials, business leaders, and laymen. Opinion surveys indicated widespread agreement with its underlying assumptions. It was consistent with theories of management that were influential in the private sector; for example, deregulate, cut middle management, make every branch a self-governing unit but hold each accountable for its profits. It was pragmatic. It was faithful to a growing body of research showing that variations in education spending and other inputs could not be counted upon to produce improved results. And it spared laymen from having to choose among competing theories of teacher education and other such matters of arcane disputation by experts.

For this schema to work, however, two ingredients are plainly essential: clear goals and standards, setting forth with precision the results that are sought; and tests that yield a steady flow of reliable feedback about the progress being made toward those goals by students, schools, states, and so on. Absent either of those elements—and it is no great exaggeration to say that U.S. education in the 1980s lacked both—such a strategy cannot be carried out.

Tests were thus indispensable, not because they directly alter behavior or cause more learning by themselves, but because tests or something similar are the vital link in any goal-based, results-driven accountability system. They are akin to the data that go onto the scoreboard and tell players and spectators which team is winning and how much time is left in the quarter. They are the lab results that tell a doctor whether a patient's blood gases and cholesterol are within proper limits. They are the speedometer that provides feedback on rate of travel, the altimeter that lets the pilot know whether the plane will clear that mountain range, the paring knife incision that shows whether the filet is rare or well done.

All this presupposes that the goals have been set, that performance standards are clear, and that all concerned are more interested in whether the field goal is scored than in how the ball is kicked. But even when those elements are present, the test is essential. Without a decent means of measurement, the objective, any objective, retains a nebulous, dreamy quality, like getting to heaven, losing weight, or wowing the crowd.

NATIONAL PROBLEM, NATIONAL SOLUTION

The standards and accountability model of education reform can operate at any level: school, district or state, as well as nation. It has come
to play an important role in reform efforts at all those levels. (And
resistance to it is vigorous at every level.)

The relationship between education and nation that existed about
1980 can be described in two strikingly different ways. With respect to
governance, management, finance, and formal responsibility, U.S.
public schooling was highly decentralized. More than 90 percent of the
(huge) tax revenues sluicing through it came from state and local
sources. Each state had its own constitutional arrangements, its own
laws and regulations, and its own decisionmaking and management
apparatus. Fifteen thousand local boards and superintendents ran the
public schools. (Some twenty-seven thousand private schools were
even more independent.) The federal government paid for a number
of special programs (each with its own rules), worried about civil
rights, sponsored research and gathered statistics but—save for a
handful of schools serving Native Americans, military dependents,
and other distinctive cases—made practically none of the key decisions about what would be taught, how, and by whom. The federal
government set no graduation requirements, hired no teachers, selected no textbooks and conferred no diplomas.

Meanwhile, the nation was remarkably homogeneous in what was
happening in classrooms and was learned by children. This was not
because of the federal government, but because dozens of other powerful influences fostered sameness from Portland, Maine, to Portland,
Oregon: teacher unions, national curriculum groups, and a handful of
powerful textbook (and test) publishers; accrediting bodies and the
two big organizations that dominated the college admissions process;
mass-circulation professional journals and similar methods of teacher
education; the profound influence of national media, Hollywood, and
the music industry; and school practices that, over the years, had
swept the nation (for example, biology in tenth grade, U.S. history in
eleventh, graduation at the end of twelfth, the 180-day school year, and
kindergarten at age five).

By 1980 American education was schizophrenic: decentralized in its
formal arrangements and its rhetoric of local control, yet strikingly uni-

form in most of its ideas and practices. What then happened was that Americans began to think about the national implications of a system that was not working well—dissatisfaction with economic productivity and competitiveness; dismay over such woes as school violence, dropouts, drugs, and teen pregnancy; and weakening civic institutions and cultural values. Distinguished people and panels subsequently reported that the nation was "at risk." It was not just Alabama or Wisconsin, not merely Omaha or Charlotte; it was the entire nation.

A national problem would seem to call for a national solution. And insofar as a sound strategy for tackling that problem depended on elements such as goals, standards, and tests, it began to be imaginable that perhaps these, too, could be worked out for the entire country.

AMERICA'S LOVE-HATE RELATIONSHIP WITH TESTS

The goals part of the formula proved relatively easy. The standards part has been more contentious but is under way. The testing part, however, turned out to reach beyond the bounds of the politically practical. Many factors contributed, and numerous individuals and groups played significant roles. The stage on which this drama unfolded is a country with strong feelings—and considerable ambivalence—toward testing.

Testing is done all the time, in practically every domain of life. America likely does more testing of people and things than any other nation. Yet surveys indicate widespread public support for still more testing, even national testing. In 1993, for example, Gallup found 70 percent of Americans favoring the use of "standardized national tests" to "determine if a student advances to the next grade level," 72 percent wanting such instruments used "to rank the local public schools in terms of student achievement," and a full 91 percent supporting their use "to identify areas in which students need extra help."[3] Despite the palpitations that each of those three words—*standardized, national, tests*—sends through the cardiovascular systems of many educators, academics, and local officials, the electorate is unabashed in its willingness to see them used.

Reliance on tests bespeaks the American faith in merit and limitless opportunity, unbounded by parental lineage, schools attended, or race. Even though tests are often used to rank, sort, and grade, most

Americans perceive them as fair and objective in ways that other judgment systems are not. Tests are thought of as giving everyone the same chance to prove themselves. You do not have to be the teacher's pet, or bribe the admissions officer, or get your uncle to call the personnel director, so long as whatever decision being made about you is based on your test results.

Acceptance of tests also has something to do with mistrust of other indicators. Is a child's report card devalued by grade inflation? Clouded by the teacher's attitude toward him? Is the superintendent being truthful about the performance of the local schools, considering that he is also seeking a larger budget from the town council?

Tests help satisfy the craving for second opinions and outside validations. Several bids are made on the new patio before a contractor is engaged. Another orthopedist is consulted before back surgery is agreed to. A new restaurant is even more enjoyable when what a diner's taste buds say is echoed by a favorable newspaper review. In education, test results play a similar role, confirming or challenging personal conclusions about a matter, buttressing or undermining what the first source said.

Comparability matters, too, both because Americans have a nose for competition and because they tend to evaluate themselves and their institutions in relation to others. (This explains the excitement generated by league rankings, play-offs, national champions, blue ribbons at the fair, the Olympics, Oscars, Emmys, Grammys, and Pulitzers.) In education, parents want to know how their child's school measures up to others in town. Melissa may be near the top of her class at Franklin Middle School, but how is she doing compared with students her age around the country? Which of the seventh-grade teachers at Franklin does the best job? How does a particular state stack up against the rest of the nation? As for the nation, is it gaining on the Koreans yet? Is it true that Hungarian children outstrip Americans in math? That U.S. science scores are equivalent to those of Kazakhstan?

Test results help allay those hungers. They also facilitate accountability. Are Americans getting their money's worth from the local schools? Should that principal be replaced? Have the incumbent mayor's policies accomplished what he promised?

Americans, however, also harbor doubts about tests and their uses. Laymen's doubts typically involve concern for their own children (Josh has good grades, works hard, and his teachers like him, but he does not test well), apprehension about a group to which they belong (Is that test biased against Polish-Americans?), or doubts about the veracity of test results themselves (Did a West Virginia doctor prove that most state and local school systems report misleading test scores?).

Most educators are far more dubious than laymen. Their skittishness toward tests and testing arises from at least five sources:

—Many hold philosophies of education that are fairly termed "progressive": child-centered, flexible, democratic, inclined to help children learn what they want to learn, when they are ready to learn it, in the ways that they learn it best, not to pressure, manipulate, dictate, compare, or be judgmental.

—Many are kindly individuals, possessing generally liberal political and social values, wary of labeling anybody, apprehensive lest they or their school do anything to disadvantage someone or cause them anxiety, enormously sensitive to the plight of at-risk youngsters, and inclined to exonerate individuals and groups from direct responsibility for their own performance, instead blaming various social, familial, political, and economic conditions for educational results.

—Educators voice particular criticisms of the tests most commonly required by state and local authorities, especially when they affect curriculum and instruction. "Teaching to the test" is seen as a sin in the United States. (One of Lauren B. Resnick's valuable insights is that many other countries have tests "worth teaching to.") Standardized tests are seen as flawed efforts to sunder complex human tasks into meaningless bits. Testing is viewed as a way of passing judgment, not improving what is taught and learned. Among analysts who specialize in testing and measurement, moreover, a strong tendency exists to find technical flaws in every known test, testing procedure, and test-linked standard-setting procedure. Their conclaves, professional journals, and congressional testimony are full of fretful, cryptic references to "validity," "reliability," "generalizability," and so on.

—The link between testing and accountability-for-results is understandably worrisome to those whose results are on the line and whose careers are involved. Teacher unions, administrator groups, and others proffer many explanations of why this or that test is unfair, why people in school ought not be held responsible for results that are also shaped by home and neighborhood, why comparisons should not be made, why external assessments are disruptive and unhelpful compared with teacher-designed evaluations, why nobody's salary or job security should be affected by what stanine their students' scores fall into, and why the voters should pass the bond issue despite the town's drooping test results.

—In keeping with their nervousness about the standards and accountability model of education reform, many professionals embrace a different paradigm: expand educational services (for example, preschool, health clinics); equalize resources among schools, districts, and states; make much greater provision for staff development; employ new technologies; concentrate on innovative instructional strategies (for example, cooperative learning); develop new curricula and curriculum frameworks and align these with textbooks, teacher training, and innovative forms of authentic assessment. This approach, which has come to be known as systemic reform, sees little or no place for conventional tests and testing.[4]

THE SURPRISING RISE OF NATIONAL TESTING . . .

Tests and testing would be hotly debated even if the word *national* had never been affixed. By the late 1980s, however, a number of people were arguing for a single set of standards and a single examination system for the entire country.

The most visible and consequential development was the education "summit" that President Bush and the governors held in Charlottesville, Virginia, in September 1989. It resulted in agreement "for the first time in U.S. history, to establish clear, national performance goals" and to "report annually on progress in achieving [the] goals."[5]

Given ingrained assumptions about local control of education and the evolution of American federalism, this was a striking development. However, these senior elected officials were ratifying a consensus that had already begun to form. Prominent educators such as Albert Shanker of the American Federation of Teachers, Ernest Boyer of the Carnegie Foundation for the Advancement of Teaching, and Marshall S. Smith of Stanford University, had called for national standards. The National Council of Teachers of Mathematics was well down the path of creating precisely such standards for its field.

Author E. D. Hirsch, Jr., had recommended that every young

American should become "culturally literate" and dared to list the information that he judged suitable for nationwide teaching and learning. Even the Council of Chief State School Officers, long-time bastion of state autonomy, was coming to embrace common standards and comparable test results.

Resistance might have been expected from Republicans, conservatives, and other traditional defenders of local control, diversity, and choice in education. But many of them had come to view state and local education systems as hopelessly enslaved by the establishment; had adopted the standards, accountability, and results strategy for reform; were reassured by the long-term hold that the GOP seemed to have on the White House; and were excited by models of what sound national standards might look like, such as those in Hirsch's book and those promulgated by William J. Bennett when he was secretary of education. They recognized, moreover, that the success of any voucher system or other school choice scheme would depend in considerable part on parental access to solid, comparable test results.

In early 1990 Bush and the governors unveiled the six national education goals that they had developed for the country. The third, for example, of these declared that "by the year 2000, American students will leave grades four, eight, and twelve having demonstrated competency over challenging subject matter, including English, mathematics, science, history and geography."[6] How would headway toward this goal (or toward the fourth goal, which vowed that young Americans would become "first in the world in science and mathematics achievement") be measured? More precise standards were needed, spelling out what challenging subject matter would be in, say, fourth-grade math or twelfth-grade geography and also prescribing the quality of performance ("how good is good enough?") that youngsters must demonstrate to be said to have attained competency. Additionally, some kind of testing or assessment system would be needed to track and report on their—and the nation's—progress.

Just how these might be devised was not clear at first. A White House press release in January 1990 asserted that "progress . . . must be measured accurately and adequately, and reported to the American people on a timely basis. . . . The President and the Governors agree that this effort will require a substantial national commitment over several years to further develop and refine . . . national measurement capabilities."[7] By July the summit participants were ready to create a

National Education Goals Panel that would be responsible for "determining the indicators used to measure the national education goals and reporting progress toward their achievement." At its inception, this new body consisted of four representatives of the federal executive branch (including Education Secretary Lamar Alexander and White House domestic aide Roger Porter) and six (bipartisan) governors.

Meanwhile, the idea of a new national test (or perhaps several of them) was winning more adherents. A White House advisory council comprised of business and education leaders was considering—and presently recommended—that new national testing programs be established with federal leadership. (The president should "cause to be developed at least two" was the artful phrasing.) A privately financed group led by scholars Lauren Resnick and Mark Tucker launched the New Standards Project, dedicated to the creation—and voluntary but nationwide use—of a fresh set of educator-devised standards that would be linked with innovative assessments and made inseparable from curriculum and instruction.

Another private organization called Educate America, headed by former New Jersey governor Tom Kean and his well-regarded education commissioner Saul Cooperman, set out to develop a new national achievement test for all high school seniors. The National Assessment of Educational Progress (NAEP) Governing Board recommended that the existing National Assessment program, which had long provided achievement data for the country as a whole and was also beginning to furnish state-level results, should be changed to enable states and localities to use NAEP test instruments to appraise student performance at the level of school districts, schools, even individual children. The federal agency responsible for education statistics issued a staff paper entitled "Implementing the National Examination System." And, by early 1991, it was not too shocking to find in the *New York Times* one Sunday morning an article by Karen DeWitt entitled "The Push to Consider a Once Taboo Subject: National School Tests," including the prophetic observation that "getting from policy circles to implementation will be a formidable task politically."[8]

The most serious expression of actual intent to accomplish that task was the Bush administration's AMERICA 2000 proposal in April 1991, particularly the inclusion of "American Achievement Tests." The president said, "We will develop voluntary—let me repeat it—we will develop voluntary national tests for 4th, 8th and 12th graders in the five core subjects. These American Achievement Tests will tell parents and educators, politicians and employers, just how well our schools are doing. I'm determined to have the first of these tests for 4th graders in place by the time that school starts in September of 1993."[9]

Yet this did not come to pass. The Bush administration never submitted a bill to Congress that would carry out the president's commitment. In retrospect, that April day in the East Room was the high watermark of the national testing idea, at least any version of it bearing a relationship to the federal government. It has been sinking ever since. Today, it is totally submerged.

. . . AND ITS RAPID FALL

What happened instead, in the late spring and early summer of 1991, was that the administration and congressional leaders agreed to form a commission to study the idea. The National Council on Education Standards and Testing (NCEST) was a compromise and a delaying tactic, but it was also an effort to forge greater consensus about something that had rapidly become contentious.

The controversy had—and has—multiple sources. In political terms, however, the proximate origins of NCEST were vigorous resistance to the president's proposals by at least one key governor and several influential House Democrats.

The governor was Colorado's Roy Romer, a Democrat who headed the new National Education Goals Panel, which was charged with monitoring progress toward the national goals but which had gotten off to a rocky start, not least because of its organizationally awkward and politically delicate relationship with—yet total financial dependence on—the Bush administration. Mercurial, energetic, education-minded, and partisan, Romer was also an early member of the board of the New Standards Project, which had received millions of foundation dollars to develop its own standards and assessment system for the country.[10] New Standards arose on the systemic reform side of the excellence movement, not the standards and accountability side. Hence philosophic differences arose between it and the Bush AMERICA 2000 proposal, which was unabashedly rooted in the latter school of thought. There may also have been a touch of jealousy. How many new national standards and assessment systems could the country take seriously? Moreover, a distinguishing characteristic of New Standards was its aversion to the federal government. Leaders of the project made no secret of their opposition to the American Achievement Test idea—and their horror at the prospect of expanding NAEP, many of whose features they appeared not to understand. Little doubt exists that Romer had this, among several considerations, on his mind when, in the spring of 1991, he stormed into White House and Education Department offices and—as former administration officials recall several outbursts—said "You can't go ahead with this."

Romer, Alexander, and others had also gotten an earful or two from Representative Dale E. Kildee, the Michigan Democrat who chaired a key House education subcommittee. Kildee did not like testing. He did not like much of anything about AMERICA 2000. He did not like the Bush administration or want it to succeed. And he and his colleagues were aggrieved by having been left out of the high visibility national goals process, up to this point the exclusive province of governors and the executive branch.[11]

Capitol Hill was already threatening Alexander and company with dire legislative and fiscal consequences if they spent any more Education Department money to advance that process. Kildee was briefed by New Standards leaders and other opponents of national testing. He had numerous conversations with Romer. With the 1992 election approaching, blocking George Bush from making good on his pledge to be the "education president" was a mission dear to the hearts of more than one Democrat.

The upshot was that Alexander and his team saw no practical way to launch the American Achievement Tests quickly, either by unilateral action or through legislation. Moreover, some parts of the goals process that were even higher on their priority list—such as funding the projects that would turn the third goal into detailed, subject-by-subject standards—were in peril so long as Congress was on the warpath. Shrewd politics dictated some effort to appease and perhaps win over the critics and opponents.

Accordingly, the AMERICA 2000 bill sent to Congress on May 22 contained numerous provisions but did not provide for national standards or tests. (It would, however, have expanded NAEP, though not so far as the Governing Board had suggested.) Instead, Alexander, Romer, Kildee, and others worked out an agreement for Congress speedily to authorize NCEST, which was bipartisan, chaired by two governors (Romer, and South Carolina's Carroll A. Campbell, Jr.), included members of Congress (one of them Kildee) as well as representatives of the education community, and was charged with advising the American people on "Whether, while respecting State and local control of education, an appropriate system of voluntary national tests or examinations should and can be established."[12] NCEST began meeting in mid-summer 1991, worked hard, was brilliantly staffed, and managed to issue its report in January 1992—breakneck speed for such a commission. The panel was clear in recommending the development and use of four different kinds of standards, including national standards for subject matter content and student achievement. But when it came to testing, NCEST made a fundamental shift from the kind of single national exam that Bush and others had in mind. Instead, it urged the creation of what it termed a "system of multiple assessments linked to the national standards that will measure the progress of individuals, schools, districts, states and the Nation." Though the council's criteria for such a system included the requirement that "different assessments produce comparable results," what was envisioned was both more nebulous and more complicated than the version recommended just months earlier.

How a system of separate but comparable tests would work, or even if such a thing is technically possible, was never made clear. Eminent psychometricians contend that, unless two tests are practically identical, stating with confidence how a student (or school or state) with a certain score on one would have done on the other is very difficult.[13] Particularly if policymakers want to attach high stakes to student and school results, the burden may be heavier than a loosely knit confederation of separate tests can sustain. If an employer decides to hire Thelma instead of Louise because of the former's superior score on an achievement test, the choice is apt to be defensible if they took the same test. But what if they took different tests that had purportedly been equated or linked to each other? In a litigious society such as America's, one suspects that the employer will need persuasive evidence that the equating process was technically watertight. But that, many testing experts say, is extremely difficult to do, the more so if the tests are truly distinctive.

In any event, two years passed and no such system has come into being, nor is any on the horizon. Oversimplifying only a bit, none of

the key players in Washington seems to favor the idea anymore—
including the Clinton administration, even though Governor Clinton
had played a leading role in drafting the national goals and establishing the mechanisms by which progress toward them would be tracked,
and Clinton and Al Gore campaigned in 1992 on a pledge to "Create a
national examination system to measure our students' and schools'
progress in meeting the national standards."[14] An October 1992 article
bearing Clinton's name in a prominent education journal refers favor-
ably to "the national test" that would be part of his administration's
policy package.[15]

The newly enacted Goals 2000 legislation does nothing to create
either a national test or a system of tests, though it authorizes the
NEGP and a new standards and improvement council to certify assessments that states may, but need not, place before them. The federal
funds authorized by this measure to assist states and localities to
achieve the national goals may not be spent for any high-stakes tests.
The reasoning—that holding students accountable for results is unfair
until assurances exist that their schools are furnishing them a complete
and equitable opportunity to learn—is taken straight from the systemic reform paradigm, not the standards, testing and accountability
formula. That it has now been enshrined in the federal statute books
represents a fairly decisive victory, at least at the national level, for the
former view and an important defeat for those who believe that tests
with consequences are essential components of any education reform
destined to alter behavior and boost learning.

WHO KILLED NATIONAL TESTING?

If national testing is dead for the foreseeable future, holding an inquest
is not unreasonable. Some will say it died of natural causes: a frail, pre-
mature, or overwrought creature whose heart stopped beating. Others
see signs of homicide.

The evidence points in the latter direction. National testing was a
robust concept with immense popular support. That it perished is not
the result of a wasting disease but a gangland-style execution. The cul-
pable gang consists of five factions, overlapping in membership but
each with its own motives.

First is what may be termed the traditional antitesting crowd, those individuals and organizations that have tried to make the SAT go away, have fought every extension of NAEP, have objected when states required high school students to pass minimum competency tests before getting a diploma, and so on. Civil rights organizations are prominent here, as are educators nervous about accountability, idealists who believe that education should be motivated by love of learning instead of fear of being found ignorant, and a strident advocacy group known as FairTest, which is to educational testing as People for the Ethical Treatment of Animals (PETA) is to biomedical research. The reaction against all forms of testing was intensified by the fact that Republicans were proposing this version and that, barring an uncertain change in control of the White House, the GOP might wind up with something to say about what should be on the test and what uses would be made of its results. Besides testifying in congressional hearings and rallying supporters to write their representatives, members of this crowd characteristically call a press conference or take out a newspaper advertisement to publicize an "open letter to the president" (or whomever), signed by dozens of people, denouncing the latest proposal and declaring that it, like all extant forms of testing, would be bad for children, minorities, and other living creatures.

Second are conservatives fearful of federal control of education, anxious about the fate of private schools (and home-schoolers) in a more heavily regulated education system, nervous about the large role of testing in outcome-based education, worried that the whole process of setting standards and developing tests will fall into the wrong hands (for example, multiculturalists), or opposed to education reform itself because it might make the present system more bearable, hence stave off the voucher revolution. That the notoriously moderate Bush administration was behind the idea made it even more suspect to true-blue conservatives.

Third are organizations with their own tests or plans for testing, whose status or revenues might be threatened by a national test. Competition is not necessarily their sole motivation. When the president of Educational Testing Service, the head of the College Board (now developing its own new Pacesetter program), or one of the leaders of the New Standards Project inveighed against national testing, differing belief systems were involved along with organizational self-interest. When the commercial test-publishers behaved similarly, their rationale may have been more single-minded.

Fourth are equivocal or ill-informed policymakers. Governors, Education Department officials, White House advisers, and others interested in results and accountability were jittery about a single national test. It sounded slightly Orwellian. Good reason existed to keep it separate from the federal government, yet identifying a realistic alternative structure that could develop, underwrite, and implement it was hard. Instead, the idea of several tests that states, localities, and schools could choose among was proposed. "At least two," said the President's Education Policy Advisory Council. A system of multiple tests, urged NCEST. Never mind the inherent difficulty, perhaps the impossibility, of making such a system technically sound. Those were details for the staff to work out. For those with political fingers poking the air, pluralism in this matter felt a bit more American, particularly after opposition surfaced.

Fifth is a cadre of testing experts, whose technical requirements that any test must meet before it is used for anything tend to give them permanent employment but also serve to slow and complicate the process, sometimes halting it altogether. Like a dam that cannot be built until the environmental experts satisfy themselves that no obscure subspecies of worm or ragweed will be drowned, any new test—especially any that is national or that carries the possibility of consequences—must be delayed until a few experts at Boston College, the University of California at Los Angeles, RAND, and the National Academy of Education are content with every unintended consequence that could conceivably ensue. Because, in the real world, such contentment is never attainable (at least not within the term of any sitting governor or president), the net effect of expert counsel is that nothing be done or, at minimum, that the experts be given new grants and contracts to monitor and evaluate whatever is done.

As seems usually to be the case in Washington when a policy innovation is under consideration, the status quo turned out to have more defenders than the change had advocates. The Bush administration, with numerous irons in the fire, did not press hard for national testing. The NCEST report provided cover for those who wanted something like national testing but not exactly national testing (and it offered a haven for those who did not quite understand the distinction). Articulate advocates who well understood the difference, people such as Albert Shanker, realized that Congress was a long way from being sold on the idea. (The Senate possibly would have bought it, but

Kildee and other key members of the House Education and Labor Committee were implacably opposed.) The governors kept still. The National Education Goals Panel, which would have been the most prominent user of data from national testing, kept its own counsel. The National Assessment Governing Board, already under fire for its effort to develop student performance standards for NAEP results, backed off. As so often happens, those who felt they had something to lose from the proposal were far more strongly motivated than those who stood to gain. It is not difficult to visualize the loss of something to which one is accustomed; it is harder to imagine the benefit from something one has never had.

The 1992 elections further changed the dynamics. Once in office, the Clinton administration showed little interest in testing, but considerable enthusiasm for what became known as "opportunity to learn," a concept beloved of systemic reformers though scorned by the standards and accountability crowd as a fancy new term for old-style tinkering with school inputs. Desperately wanting to enact its school reform bill—dubbed Goals 2000, to distinguish it from Bush's never-passed AMERICA 2000 proposals—the new team bent over backwards to accommodate the same members of Congress who opposed national testing, adjusting the administration's bill to suit them before it was ever dispatched to Capitol Hill. Despite the new president's campaign statements, and Education Secretary Richard W. Riley's steadfast allegiance to accountability for results when he was governor of South Carolina, the national testing idea was nowhere to be found in Goals 2000. The bill, now statute, has provisions that may even discourage states from devising their own testing and accountability programs.[16]

WHAT ABOUT NAEP?

The National Assessment of Educational Progress contains several elements of national testing: an elaborate consensus process that generates both the content standards that determine what will be on the test and the student performance standards by which results can be analyzed and reported; a regular cycle for testing student achievement in the core subjects in grades four, eight, and twelve; a nationwide test-taking population; the ability to monitor progress over time; a complicated but generally well-regarded approach to testing (for example, steadily diminishing reliance on multiple choice formats); and an independent governing board that enables this sensitive program to be federally funded without being directly under the thumb of political appointees, bureaucratic processes, or single-minded interest groups.

But NAEP also lacks several essentials. The most important is the ability to administer tests and report results at the levels where they might undergird accountability efforts, affect behavior, and, perhaps, improve achievement. NAEP tests are given primarily to a national sample of students, with results reported for the country as a whole and for its major regions. Since 1990 some NAEP tests have also been administered at certain grade levels to samples of youngsters in states that volunteered to participate in the trial state assessment (and most did). But no results are available—Congress has barred them—for local school systems or individual schools, let alone for individual students. Hence the primary objective of a national test—giving parents clear feedback on how their children and their school are doing—cannot be met by NAEP as presently conceived. Moreover, the authority and funding for state-by-state assessments are precarious. Given recent appropriation levels and the Clinton administration's budget assumptions, not more than one or two subjects will be tested at the state level in each biennial assessment cycle for the rest of the 1990s.

NAEP is also under attack from a host of foes, some of them the same as the enemies of national testing. The 103d Congress attempted to eliminate or emasculate its independent governing board. There are several reasons for this; most important is that the board has persevered in its effort to develop student performance standards (achievement levels, in NAEP parlance) by which to report national and state results. These standards have the effect of transforming a neutral, boring, nonjudgmental body of data, used primarily by analysts and researchers, into a means of tracking progress toward the third national goal with the help of clear judgments about how well students ought to be doing. And that is precisely why many people do not like them.

At least three of the five factions of the national testing assassination squad have tried to make the Governing Board cease and desist or, failing that, lose its ability to make binding policy decisions. They largely succeeded in the House in early 1994. How the Senate will respond remains to be seen.

PROSPECTS FOR THE YEARS AHEAD

As an endeavor involving the federal government, national testing is dead for the foreseeable future. This may seem strange, given ample evidence of the depth and sincerity of public support for the idea and its indispensability in any serious effort to monitor (and leverage) progress toward the national education goals. But the public is not always well served by those it elects to office, nor by experts who set themselves up to second guess what is good for the citizenry. Education reform has been such a field for at least a decade, and national testing may be the premier example of the ability of a handful of individuals to dominate an important decision.

Some states will continue to do their own thing, perhaps gearing their assessments to the slowly emerging national content standards. (It appears that no national student performance standards will be developed for years to come, save for those developed by NAGB, which are in acute political peril.)

In terms of placing accountability where it matters and leveraging behavioral change in students and schools, state-level testing is fine. National testing was never needed for this purpose. Comparability is what is lost when each state acts independently, along with certain other benefits associated with interstate parity in education standards.

One or two states have secured permission from the federal government to equate or link their assessments with NAEP. To the extent that this practice spreads—and proves technically sound—comparability will increase. But the roots of state-based testing may not turn out to be very deep, either. High-quality assessments are expensive to develop. And the absence of a national test means much duplication and redundancy, perhaps more than state legislators will want to bear.

Commercial testmakers will attempt to profit from national standards. (Some tests are already advertised as being based on the standards of the National Council of Teachers of Mathematics.) Prosperity may also befall ventures such as the College Board's Pacesetter program. The New Standards Project will doubtless persevere with its ambitious effort to create national exams worth teaching to, although leaders of that project seem far more interested in affecting the instructional process than in accountability or comparability. Their primary clients are educators, not policymakers, business leaders, or parents.

For the most part, parents will continue to lack prompt, accurate, intelligible data about how their children (applicants, schools, and so on) are doing. Crucially missing will be the ability to relate the performance of their children, schools, communities, and states to anything larger—the rest of the country and the world.

CONCLUSION

A high price will be paid for this information shortfall. Achievement of the national education goals is less likely. Without tests that put them to use, less need will exist for student performance standards, which the developers of content standards are only too willing to defer into the distant future. Absent such standards and achievement data keyed to them, education reform is putty in the hands of both those on the right who want to torpedo the notion of outcomes and those on the left who would return to input standards.

Those who might have a catalytic effect on schools and students, notably universities and employers, will find it harder to be taken seriously and thus to alter behavior. Parents will be less able to monitor the education of their children and to make wise choices among schools. They will continue to assume the schools their children attend are doing a fine job, a supposition that plays right into the hands of the reform-averse education establishment. Education will be held less accountable for their successes and failures, as the American tendency to treat education as a no-fault endeavor in which nobody is responsible for much of anything will continue.

The demise of national testing is not the whole story. Plenty of factors contribute to the lackluster performance of American education, the general failure of post–1983 reform efforts to yield stronger results, and the system's staunch resistance to change. But the excellence movement will not grind to a complete halt. Some of its latest manifestations are bolder than ever: voucher schemes, charter schools, the contracting-out of school management to private operators, the spread of "break-the-mold" school designs, states wiping out their entire education code and rewriting it from scratch, and so on.

Such efforts will likely continue and perhaps intensify, putting deeper and wider cracks into the foundation on which the public education establishment rests uneasily. National testing would have accelerated these processes of change, mainly by giving parents and voters far better data on school results than most of them can put their hands on today. Lacking such information, they will be less discerning and perhaps less demanding.

Some of this information can come from other sources, however, and most likely it will. America's appetite for test results will somehow be sated, whether with the psychometric equivalent of junk food or with something more nutritious. Those who blocked national testing in the early 1990s may awake one day to find widespread use of instruments they like even less. And in the fullness of time—and the cycle of elections—the possibility remains that the idea of national testing will itself reappear, perhaps stronger than before, thanks to the exercise it has had on the obstacle course it has been obliged to run.

NOTES

1. John Jacob Cannell, *Nationally Normed Elementary Achievement Testing in America's Public Schools: How All Fifty States Are Above the National Average* (Daniels, W.Va.: Friends for Education, 1987), pp. 1–2.

2. National Governors' Association, *Time for Results* (Washington, 1986), p. 3.

3. Stanley M. Elam, Lowell C. Rose, and Alec M. Gallup, "The 25th Annual Phi Delta Kappa/Gallup Poll," *Phi Delta Kappan,* vol. 75 (October 1993), pp. 137–52.

4. This is a recent development. Just a few years ago, many leading proponents of systemic reform, such as Bill Honig and Marshall Smith, were arguing for a model in which testing played a key role. Unfortunately, this movement has been hijacked by people and groups for whom tests, at least the kind with consequences, are anathema.

5. *The President's Education Summit with Governors* (Charlottesville, Va.: Department of Education, September 27–28, 1989), appendix A, p. 1.

6. Department of Education, *America 2000: An Education Strategy Sourcebook* (Washington, April 1991), p. 62.

7. White House press release, January 31, 1990, cited in *President's Education Summit with Governors,* appendix B.

8. Karen DeWitt, "The Push to Consider a Once Taboo Subject: National School Tests," *New York Times,* February 3, 1991.

9. Department of Education, *America 2000,* p. 5.

10. For a blunt appraisal of Governor Roy Romer's temperament and motives by a White House aide who saw him up close, see Charles Kolb, *White House Daze* (Free Press, 1994), especially pp. 139–40.

11. Strictly speaking, members of Congress had already been invited to serve as nonvoting members of the National Education Goals Panel, but this did not mollify them.

12. National Council on Education Standards and Testing, *Raising Standards for American Education* (Washington: Department of Education, January 24, 1992), p. B–2.

13. Robert L. Linn, "Linking Results of Distinct Assessments," University of Colorado at Boulder, Center for Research on Evaluation, Standards, and Student Teaching.

14. Bill Clinton and Al Gore, *Putting People First: How We Can All Change America* (Times Books, 1992), pp. 85–86.

15. Bill Clinton, "The Clinton Plan For Excellence in Education," *Phi Delta Kappan*, vol. 74 (October 1992), p. 135.

16. This is a complicated piece of legislation with a mixture of incentives and disincentives, the combined impact of which will not be clear for years.

ALBERT SHANKER

The Case for High Stakes and
Real Consequences

Some danger exists that world class standards will become America's latest education slogan. At a celebration following the signing of the Goals 2000 legislation, buttons, brochures, and placards everywhere proclaimed "World Class Standards." And probably committees will soon be forming in schools across the country creating their own world class standards, which will be a few notches above what they have now. But there is a world out there. America can find out about the standards to which other advanced industrialized countries hold their students if it is serious in wanting to emulate them. They are not state secrets.

One way of coming at these standards is to look at the examinations students in other countries are expected to pass. A 1994 publication of the American Federation of Teachers and the National Center for Improving Science Education, *What College-Bound Students Abroad Are Expected to Know about Biology: Exams from England and Wales, France, Germany, and Japan, Plus a Comparative Look at the United States,* describes the examinations that qualify students for university entrance in each of these countries and gives examples of actual examinations, as well as an Advanced Placement (AP) biology exam from the United States.

The AP is a respectable exam; it is not a pushover. But most Americans who look at the exams that college-bound students in other countries have to pass will probably wish that American kids could reach a similar level before going on to college—and not only in biology but in many subjects. Students in other countries do not reach high levels of achievement simply because someone has created a tough exam. The examination is part of an educational system that includes a common curriculum, either within individual states or within the country, and standards that students work to meet as they prepare for the exams.

However, this description leaves out a critical element in the successful education systems of other advanced industrial democracies. Stakes are attached to meeting the standards: Students work hard to pass difficult examinations because they cannot get into college without doing so. The same goes for students who are going into the job market or on for technical training. They work hard to pass different but equally demanding exams so they can qualify for good jobs, apprenticeships or technical training programs. Unless stakes become part of the debate in the United States—unless what students do in school is connected with what they hope to do after they graduate—world class standards and sophisticated techniques for developing curriculum and assessments will not mean a thing.

One objection that is often raised to looking seriously at school systems in other advanced industrial democracies is that their systems are elitist while America's is egalitarian and educates all comers. This may once have been true of the education systems in France or Germany or England, but it is no longer, and the percentage of youngsters in each of these countries who take the biology examinations and pass them makes this fact plain. In the United Kingdom, 31 percent of students take the exam; 43 percent in France and 37 percent in Germany. In Japan, counting the first and second tries, 58 percent of students take it. In the United States, only 7 percent of students take the Advanced Placement exam in biology. What about the students who pass it? Twenty-five percent in the United Kingdom; 32 percent in France; 36 percent in Germany; 36 percent in Japan; 4 percent in the United States.

The number of such exams students in the various countries have to take to qualify for college is also significant. College applicants in the United Kingdom have to pass three; in France seven or eight; in Germany four; in Japan three or four. And youngsters applying to college in the United States? They do not have to pass any exam testing their mastery of subject matter.

Which system is elitist? The one where only a tiny fraction of youngsters take and pass an examination—undoubtedly the kids whose parents graduated from college and who are headed for elite colleges themselves—or one where one-third to one-half of all students graduating from high school take a number of such exams and 25 to 35 percent pass them? And what accounts for the discrepancy between the few students achieving at high levels in the U.S. egalitarian system and the much larger percentage in the supposedly elitist systems of other advanced industrial democracies?

Although the rigorous and well-understood standards and the curriculum and exams designed to reflect these standards are important, they do not, by themselves, account for the discrepancy. Instead, it is the failure to have standards and stakes that leads to elitism—to a system where few succeed except for a small group of youngsters who have a lot going for them.

If officials in Germany or Japan announced next year that graduating seniors could get into university without passing any of these examinations, would students take the exams in the numbers they do now, and would they study as hard to pass them? Would the announcement have any effect on how much homework students did (in comparison with the time they spent watching TV and playing video games)? Would it have any effect on whether their teachers pressed ahead to give students a thorough grounding in everything on the syllabus or spent time on other things that had nothing to do with preparing for the exams?

When I was teaching and assigned a quiz or an essay, I always knew the first question that the students would ask: "Does it count?" Does it count? The United States has an educational system in which very little counts. And as long as it does not matter whether kids meet certain agreed-on standards in math or chemistry or American history, students will do the least amount possible to get the only thing that does count—that piece of paper, the diploma. The only exception to this rule are youngsters who want to go to elite colleges. There are stakes—and there are consequences—for these kids, so they work hard to get what they want.

School reformers who are working to solve the problem of students' low achievement levels have come up with all sorts of new and creative things, but as long as students are given no reason to work, it is hard to see how any reform, however ingenious or creative, will achieve what is needed. The absence of stakes makes the whole system trivial.

This oversight is odd in a country known for developing the philosophy called pragmatism. Europeans and Asians do not really understand pragmatism, and John Dewey, William James, and Charles Sanders Peirce have never been popular elsewhere in the world. Yet, when it comes to trying to change schools, America is unpragmatic and unintelligent in its approach.

Some people try to explain the differences in achievement between U.S. schools and the successful systems of other advanced industrialized democracies by saying that they have homogeneous populations, which are easier to educate. This (like the business about elitist education systems) used to be true, but, with the exception of Japan, it is no longer. In the aftermath of colonialism, both England and France have large numbers of immigrants from former territories. And Germany has many immigrant workers and refugees.

These countries do not all have the same problems; nor do they have school systems that are identical. But they are enough like each other—and like the United States—for problems and solutions to be generally applicable. And in their systems 35 to 40 percent of the youngsters go to college because they have met tough standards not, as with American kids, because 95 percent of the colleges have no standards.

Furthermore, these other industrial democracies do not stop with educating 40 percent of their young people to a high level. Their education systems also offer a worthwhile curriculum to the 60 percent who are not going on to college. This means that they engage in tracking, a practice that many Americans consider a capital crime in education. However, the United States also tracks. The difference is that tracking here means that college-bound students get a good education whereas youngsters in other tracks get nothing of value. It is not tracking that is evil; it is what is done with kids once they are categorized that is evil—or good.

Americans often use what they consider to be good business practice as the basis for advice to schools. So perhaps they should ask themselves how the owners of a successful business would behave if, after being in operation for a number of years, they suddenly found that they were being overtaken by their competitors. Undoubtedly, one of the first things would be to look at the other businesses' operations and try to figure out why the competitors were now being more successful. They might even try to hire some of their competitors' employees. Why doesn't it occur to Americans to apply this strategy to the failure in the education system? Doing that would not mean copying every detail of the education systems in other countries. But the United States would probably follow them pretty closely, especially to begin with.

What is it that they have? First, many of them have a common curriculum. America seems to have decided against a common curriculum because people fear it would be coercive, but the question will need to be revisited because the mobility of American families creates some special problems for the education system.

Students cannot be prepared to pass an examination as tough as the ones represented in the American Federation of Teachers and the National Center for Improving Science Education report without using every available minute of school time. However, if the United States has fifty different systems, teachers will never be sure what newcomers in the class have studied, so they will do exactly what they do now—which is to spend about 30 percent of the class time reviewing the material from the previous year before moving ahead with the current year's work. American students already spend less time in school than students in other advanced industrial democracies, and a system—or rather nonsystem—that leads to wasting a large amount of the class time is something that should be looked at carefully.

I strongly supported the Goals 2000 legislation because it gets people talking about and debating standards and assessments. But without stakes, reform will not go anywhere: The kids will not take it seriously and neither will the teachers.

Under the current system, most teachers have a good deal of freedom when it comes to curriculum. When I began teaching in New York City, the assistant principal gave me several big books, each of which contained fifty or sixty different topics. He told me to pick whatever topics I or the students liked, and if I did not like any of them to make up something of my own. That was the curriculum. Teachers who are used to that kind of freedom will not be willing to follow a prescribed curriculum unless stakes are attached. If it does not make any difference whether kids learn one set of topics or another—if there are no consequences for the kids—why should teachers throw out the curriculum they have perfected over time?

Stakes for kids go right to the heart of what motivates them to work and learn. If you want someone to behave in a certain way, you connect that behavior with something the person wants. Some people reject this principle because they are offended by the view of human nature it implies. This is understandable. I, too, would prefer a world in which youngsters would open up a play by Shakespeare because they were eager to get into it instead of being forced to read the play because it is on the final examination. However, the last great experiment with a system that dismissed incentives—and relied instead on the goodness of people's instincts and motives—went down in flames recently, and the survivors are now trying to build a system based on incentives. And for most kids, unless they have to do it, they will not. This is why they are not taking the AP exams and are not achieving at the levels of youngsters in other educational systems. They do not have to work hard in school to get what they want; what they do in school has no consequences.

What is being said to children is the equivalent of telling adults, "From now on you do not have to come to work. We realize that our system has been very oppressive and many of you have resented it. So starting tomorrow you will get your pay and health plan and be eligible for pension benefits whether or not you come to work." What would be the results? A few people who love their jobs would come. A handful of compulsives would also show up, unless they decided to seek psychiatric help. The rest of the system? It would go to hell. That is what has been done with youngsters. They have been told that they can get their pay and pension and health plan without ever showing up for work. Given the set-up of the education system, they do not have to learn, they do not have to do anything.

So how much students learn turns into how much the teacher can force them to learn. And the teacher who expects a lot of students becomes a villain. Students complain. They say the teacher down the hall and the teacher they had last year and the one who is teaching their sister or brother does not assign this much work, so why is their teacher doing it? The teacher is then in the position of having to negotiate with the students because they know that no one in the outside world requires anything of them. This was all laid out in *The Shopping Mall High School,* and it is just as true in U.S. high schools now as it was in 1985. However, the same cannot be said of the educational systems in other advanced industrial democracies.

In these countries, all the teachers at a given level are assigning similar kinds of work because their students are all heading for the same assessments. If the kids were to tell the teacher that he was assigning too much work, the answer would be easy: The teacher would be able to say that he was giving students what all the other teachers give their students, not only in this school but throughout the state or the country. And he could tell them that he knew they could do it because all the kids last year did it and the year before and the year before that. "Besides," he would say, "I am here to help you. I am your coach."

That standard is external to a particular teacher or school, and having it in place entirely changes the relationship between teachers and youngsters. It also changes the relationship between parents and children. When American parents today tell their children to work harder, the kids ask why. They point out that most colleges do not care and their school does not care either. Authority has been taken away from teachers and parents, so pleading and begging are required to get children to work. A system of stakes would return that authority.

Is there any doubt that if 36 percent of the kids in another industrialized democracy can pass something at least as difficult as an Advanced Placement examination—and probably much harder—that 36 percent of U.S. kids can do it? Would it make a difference for those youngsters and the nation? Would it make a difference to higher education? There is no question that it would.

High standards would have to be phased in. If they were established tomorrow, nearly all institutions of higher education would have to shut down or be turned into junior high schools or high schools.

And what about the youngsters who, if real standards were in place, would no longer make it to college? This is a tough question. Under the present system, going to college is an entitlement. Any effort to raise admission standards and say that an applicant needs knowledge or skill or even native ability to get into college would be viewed as a way of cutting off access and opportunity. But under a system with standards and stakes, more youngsters would achieve more—remember the 36 percent of graduating seniors who pass a tough exam in Germany—and more would probably graduate from college. In countries where college students have to pass rigorous exams, no 50 percent college dropout rate exists the way it does in the United States. In Germany, for example, 83 percent of those who are admitted to college also graduate. More American high school graduates go to college, but many do not stay. These youngsters are not being granted any favors by pretending that they are prepared to do college work.

Instituting real standards for college entry does not mean abandoning the youngsters who are not headed for college. In other advanced industrial democracies, these kids have access to other programs that prepare them for getting a job, apprenticeships, or further technical training. And grades count in these other programs. The connections between school and work are as direct as the ones between school and college: Everybody is heading down a well-defined path toward an important goal.

However, even if companies that typically hire high school kids decided to connect school performance with work by hiring the best students first, they would have a hard time under the current system. Without some kind of national standards, it would be impossible to know whether one teacher's A meant the same thing as another teacher's A. Also, high schools are not accustomed to getting transcripts out in a few days—six months is more typical—and transcripts are designed with college admission in mind, not employment. If those problems were solved and if every kid in high school knew that getting a job depended on being a good student, would that make more students work hard in school? No question about it. But employers would be unlikely to adopt this hiring policy for a couple of reasons.

One is the civil rights laws. If a McDonald's manager decides to hire a kid who has gotten straight A's to work punching a cash register that has pictures of Big Macs on it and thereby denies an opportunity to a poor kid or a minority kid, is that fair? Is it legal? Other countries do not have this problem. They just assume that an employer will hire the applicant who is the best qualified regardless of the applicant's race, gender, or ethnic group. Employers in other countries deliberately seek students who have excellent school records because they feel that rewarding that kind of effort helps make the school system work and thus is part of their social responsibility. Companies follow the same procedure when they hire high school graduates, and they are able to take the grades seriously because the grades represent how well the student measured up to recognized standards of performance.

In the United States, high school graduates who go right into the job market know that, whether or not they did well in school, no good company will hire them when they are eighteen or nineteen years of age. These companies prefer to let new graduates get their first jobs elsewhere. Then when the employees are twenty-four or twenty-five, companies can hire the ones who have shown they are good workers. So the new graduates who work hard and do well end up getting the same poor jobs as the kids who did no work at all. And guess which kid looks at the other and says, "Sucker!"

World class standards and curriculum and assessments based on these standards will be no more successful than any other reform unless stakes are attached to the assessments. Stakes change everything. They change the teacher's relationship to students and the parents' relationship to their children. They mean that school boards and superintendents would be less likely to go for fads because they would know that what went on in school really counted in the future of their students. And if community members knew that students' ability to get into college or to get a job depended on how well the system did, a much higher level of public concern and support for education would exist because the current system says: "School does not count; it does not make any difference whether your kid passes or does not pass. He can go to college. No employer is ever going to look at this transcript." The U.S. education system is dysfunctional because it is disconnected from the world of work and from postsecondary education, and as long as it is disconnected, no kind of reform, however intelligent or intelligently pursued, will work.

DANIEL M. KORETZ

Sometimes a Cigar Is Only a Cigar, and Often a Test Is Only a Test

Chester E. Finn, Jr., blames five groups of people for the death of national testing initiatives. The fifth group that deserves blame—or credit—is what Finn calls a cadre of testing experts. He refers to

> a cadre of testing experts whose technical requirements that any test must meet before it is used for anything tend to give them permanent employment but also serve to slow and complicate the process, sometimes halting it all together. Like a dam that cannot be built until the environmental experts satisfy themselves that no obscure subspecies of worm or rag weed will be drowned, any new test—especially any that is national or that carries the possibility of consequences—must be delayed until a few experts at Boston College, the University of California at Los Angeles, RAND, and the National Academy of Education are content with every unintended consequence that could conceivably ensue.

George Madaus of Boston College, undoubtedly one of the unnamed experts, sent me via the Internet a two-sentence response with which I would like to start my comments. He wrote: "I never realized that pupils were 'an obscure subspecies of worm or ragweed.' If I had known that, I never would have opposed a national test."

Donald M. Stewart did a wonderful job of talking about the need for balance between enthusiasm, on the one hand, and realism and respect for evidence, on the other. That balance has been woefully lacking in the reform movement over the last several years, particularly with respect to the role of assessment. Enthusiasm has been abundant, and attention to and respect for hard evidence has sometimes been in short supply. What some testing experts, including myself, have been trying to do is not to voice skepticism but simply to put the balance back where it belongs, to reintroduce realistic expectations and a healthy respect for empirical evidence into discussions about the role of assessment in educational reform. My goal, and that of some of my colleagues, is not to discourage reform and innovation in assessment, but to improve the odds of successful reform by avoiding unrealistic expectations and impractical policies.

The need for higher standards is obvious. I do not agree with people such as Gerald Bracey who argue that the news about the performance of American students is rosy. I recently had the humbling experience of looking through a series of Japanese college entrance exams in mathematics, which are not performance exams of the sort that Lauren B. Resnick advocates. They are short answer and multiple choice. But they are extraordinarily tough. I found that I could not solve a lot of the problems that were on an entrance exam for students in the humanities. This is another sign that America's standards are low relative to those of some other nations.

I also agree with the notion that the only way to raise standards— this is a view phrased most strongly by Theodore R. Sizer—is to have a discourse about concrete examples that show people what kinds of work students are expected to do. Assessment can play a central role in this process. I also accept that educators have a responsibility to decrease inequities in the society and that most public school systems lack effective accountability mechanisms.

Proposals are needed that address problems in the educational system realistically and that have a good chance of working. That requires that more realistic and more modest expectations are set about reform in general and about assessment in particular than those that currently permeate the policy debate.

SOMETIMES A CIGAR . . .

Sigmund Freud is reputed to have said that "Sometimes a cigar is only a cigar." He was wrong on two counts. First, most psychologists now believe that a cigar is usually just a cigar. In other words, despite this famous aphorism, Freud still overestimated the psychological valence or power of cigars and other, similarly shaped objects. Second, cigars, in terms of physiology, have much more power than many people in Freud's day understood. Biomedical scientists spent decades identifying a whole host of cytological and histological effects of cigars. People such as Finn would no doubt have called them obscure cytological and histological effects, as a way of disparaging facts that they do not fully understand and find inconvenient. However obscure these physiological effects might seem, they have proved lethal to many people. So, psychologically, a cigar is usually a cigar but it has other powers, some of which are negative, that no one fully appreciated back in Freud's time.

Tests, unlike cigars, have redeeming social value. Assessment clearly has a great deal to offer educational reform if used prudently. Moreover, a good bit is known about what assessments can and cannot do, and an appreciable amount is known about the pernicious effects that can accompany their misuse. In today's policy debate, this information often is ignored or, worse, disparaged. The information is available, however, and it ought to be used to inform policy and augmented where it is too meager.

THE LIMITS OF ASSESSMENT AS A TOOL OF REFORM

What are some of the limits of assessment and the risks of its misuse? Andrew C. Porter noted one of the concerns that has been frequently voiced about high-stakes testing: Holding students responsible for testing well on material that they have not had a reasonable chance to master is unfair. That would be punishing students for the crimes of their elders. True enough, but that is only one of many cautions that measurement experts and others have voiced over the last several years. Several additional concerns have been voiced.

First, high-stakes testing often produces an illusion of accountability and an illusion of progress. During the 1980s, when people were held accountable for performance on multiple-choice tests, the so-called Lake Wobegon effect emerged, with most states and localities reporting that they scored above average. Most states and localities cannot be above average; their scores are inflated—that is, misleading. A number of studies have been done on the size of that inflation of test scores. It can be very large. The reason is transparent. As Stewart mentioned, most tests are supposed to represent a much wider range of student performance than can possibly be put on a test. In the language of the trade, a test is usually a small sample from a broad domain of achievement. Once teachers focus on the specific content or format of a test, the test will gradually become less representative of the domain students are to master and that the test is supposed to represent. Scores will then increase more than mastery of the domain.

Second, the flip side of the focus on the content of a high-stakes test is a narrowing of instruction. Studies, for instance, have shown that elementary school teachers sometimes sharply curtail or even eliminate teaching subjects that are not tested. Within the subjects tested, teachers often reduce instruction pertaining to aspects of the curriculum that are not included on the test.

Third, teaching to the test often degrades instruction. Examples of this are available from the test-based accountability of the 1980s. Observers found, for example, excessive and stifling drill, time siphoned away from instruction for practice with test-preparation materials, and so on.

Fourth, the tests that most reformers want to use—various types of performance assessments—face some formidable technical obstacles. It is not uncommon for people to disparage the importance of these technical obstacles. Concerns such as reliability and validity may seem obscure, but that does not make them unimportant—any more than the obscurity of pharmacological research investigating the safety of medication you take makes it unimportant.

Some of these problems are solvable, but that does not mean they are solved. The first big step that needs to be taken is to recognize the seriousness of the obstacles.

New performance assessments also face some of the same difficulties that confront traditional tests. For example, the evidence suggests that, if anything, inflation of scores is likely to be more of a problem with certain types of performance assessment than it is with multiple-choice tests. There are two reasons for this. Performance on complex tasks tends to be idiosyncratic and typically does not generalize well from one task to the next. Hence, students prepared to do well on a few complex tasks will in many cases do poorly on others, making the meaning of their good performance on the few suspect. Compounding this problem is that complex performance assessments are expensive and time-consuming, so students will typically perform far fewer tasks than they would on a traditional test.

Fifth, as commonly administered, most tests reveal virtually nothing reliable about the quality of schools. That is not to say that educational quality does not affect scores. It does. Moreover, testing systems can be designed to evaluate the effectiveness of educational programs, albeit at considerable cost. But the test data commonly available to districts and states cannot adequately distinguish the impact of educational quality from the effects of many other factors, such as students' backgrounds.

Porter made reference to value added: measuring what educational programs have added to the performance students would have shown anyway. What most testing programs do not provide is a measure of value added. Typically, a district or state administers tests to whichever students happen to be present in selected grades. Testing, for example, commonly takes place in fourth or fifth grade and then in middle school, often eighth grade. Many of the students tested in eighth grade are not the same kids who were tested in fifth grade three years earlier. Moreover, they typically collect only limited information about students' backgrounds. The resulting snapshot of performance may not say anything about value added. It indicates whether a group of students is doing well but does not suggest what combination of things—family background, instruction—is causing scores to be high or low.

Certainly, schools exist where scores are either higher or lower than they otherwise would be because of the quality of educational programs. Many educators could identify several such schools on the basis of extensive, probably first-hand, knowledge of those schools. It is very difficult, often impossible, to identify those schools simply on the basis of commonly available test scores without that sort of extensive knowledge or much more detailed data.

A sixth concern is that many reform proposals establish too many—and often conflicting—goals for assessments. Marshall S. Smith raised the issue, citing the difficulty of using the same test (1) to monitor what is going on and (2) to hold people accountable.

The conflict between these two goals—monitoring and accountability—is more than a difficulty, in that it cannot be readily solved. Many believe that, in many circumstances, the only way to monitor overall levels of performance accurately is to use a test that is not used for accountability and therefore is not taught to in ways that might inflate scores. That is one reason that some educators vehemently oppose using the National Assessment of Educational Progress (NAEP) for local accountability. NAEP is the best and only measure of what is happening nationwide, the only representative achievement measure administered frequently. It should not be undermined by the Lake Wobegon effect.

Numerous other conflicts exist between the goals of assessment. For example, the tensions between good instruction and good assessment. It is commonly said that good instruction and good assessment are the same. That assertion is often wrong. The two sometime coincide, and assessments can be designed that more closely resemble good instruction than do, for example, multiple-choice tests. However, good instruction and good assessment are nonetheless often very different.

One of the important conflicts that can arise between good instruction and good assessment is the tension between differentiation and standardization. Good instruction often requires that teachers differentiate among their students in response to their needs, abilities, interests, motivation, or confidence. Teachers may differentiate in the selection of tasks, in the presentation of tasks, in the preparation students are given, in the time students are allowed to perform the tasks, in the amount and type of help provided to students, or in the amount of opportunity for revisions. The most capable and least capable students should not get the same versions of all tasks with the same demands. When kids vary markedly in their capabilities, presenting them all with the same tasks under the same conditions would entail either dumbing instruction down to the lowest common denominator or condemning low-ability students to frequent failure. Sometimes teachers differentiate in ways that are undesirable—for example, setting overly low expectations for less able students—but differentiation is often essential for good instruction. For example, a teacher may recognize that less able students need additional and more structured help in revising essays, while she may recognize that other students are at the point where they need to be pushed to revise without assistance.

In contrast, good assessment—good in the sense of providing information that is comparable across students—typically requires as much standardization as possible on all of these dimensions. If two students produce comparably high-quality essays, but one is a poor writer who had a lot of help with revision and the second is an able writer who had no help whatever, the comparability of their products is misleading if it is used as a basis for inferring that the students have reached comparable levels of performance.

This tension between differentiation and standardization was not as difficult an issue as long as people expected instruction and tests to be distinct activities. But the current reform movement is blurring that distinction. Many reformers call for integrating assessments into instruction, largely eliminating the distinction, and other reform proposals would institute lack of standardization for other reasons.

So, if assessment is to be embedded in or at least similar to instruction, what guidelines should teachers follow? Should they make task demands variable so that all students face challenging but manageable assignments, or should they make task demands uniform so that the quality of products means the same thing from one student or school to another? That is just one illustration of why good instruction need not be good assessment. And good assessment need not be good instruction.

The final concern is that excessive emphasis on testing and test-based accountability diverts attention from other problems, some of which are severe and pressing. Many students come to school from environments that are not conducive to good educational performance. Some come from environments that educators can barely comprehend. Some of them have not eaten. Some have never been read to. Some worry about being beaten or shot after they leave school—or even while in the school building. Some of these students can be helped by presenting them with high standards and challenging and engaging work. But it is also absurd to think that most of these kids are going to act like upper-middle-class children of Ph.D.s simply because standards have been raised and new tests are administered.

The attractiveness and simplicity of test-based accountability make it easy for people to forget that the effects of test-based accountability are going to be a relatively small drop in a large bucket. More difficult problems need to be solved—problems that require more political will than setting standards and administering tests.

COMMENTS ON CONFERENCE PARTICIPANTS' PRESENTATIONS

Lauren Resnick made the comment that, ultimately, the New Standards Project would like to rely primarily on portfolios for grading. I would like to respond with some warnings about portfolio assessment. For a number of reasons, portfolios are an extraordinarily difficult vehicle for an assessment that needs to produce comparable scores. One reason is the variations in the amount of preparation and help students receive. Another reason is that ostensibly similar tasks can be made to differ in difficulty.

In Vermont, a growing common corpus of problems exists that many teachers know and draw upon in building mathematics portfolios. Some of these problems are well enough known that they can be referred to by name: the handshake problem, the great bucket debate problem, and so on. In some cases, these problems, as implemented in the classroom, differ markedly in difficulty. For example, in the spring of 1993, one of the Vermont mathematics portfolio raters—like all raters, a math teacher himself—pointed out a common problem that, in line with the current National Council of Teachers of Mathematics emphasis on data analysis and statistics, involved combinations. He presented two instances of that same problem from portfolios he had graded. Both versions were similar in terms of almost everything except for the number of items from which students had to draw combinations. As the rater pointed out, that one difference made for a large discrepancy in the difficulty of the problems and thus undermined the comparability of scores from the schools in which those two versions were used.

Other variations in practice also pose serious obstacles to using portfolios for meaningful large-scale assessment. Teachers vary in how much of the instructional year they put into the products that are included in portfolios. They vary in terms of the amount of help that kids can get from others; as one rater said, "Whose work is this, anyway?"

Does this mean that portfolio programs are bad policy? On the contrary, they may prove to be an important tool in educators' arsenal. Vermont's portfolio assessment project, for example, is having strong positive effects on mathematics instruction. Portfolios are also a very useful tool for internal assessments; that is, assessments used within a classroom or school. Important attempts also are under way—such as the program in Vermont—to develop portfolio programs that will be useful for providing reasonably comparable performance data across schools. These are still developmental efforts, however, and until they have been shown to provide valid data for comparisons among schools and systems, serious limits will be imposed on how they should be used as part of national policy. Portfolio assessment is not yet a technology that can be relied upon to provide comparable information across school systems on a large scale. It is not yet appropriate for most systems that would impose substantial consequences on educators, and it is not yet appropriate for systems that would impose high stakes for individual students. Whether it will get to that point soon is arguable, but it is not there yet . To ignore that would be, at the very least, unfair to those students and educators who will face the consequences, and it may harm educational quality.

Chester Finn made an impassioned plea for data that would allow states to see how they stack up against the nation and would allow parents to see how their kids stack up against other kids statewide, nationwide, and even internationally. Such information is useful, but with two caveats. First, what Finn is arguing for is norm-referenced testing. Although many who disparage norm-referenced tests are treating the term as synonymous with multiple choice, norms have nothing to do with test format. Norm-referenced tests are tests that display levels of performance by comparison to some distribution of performance. International studies are basically norm-referenced: American kids are pegged on an international distribution of performance. The NAEP Trial State Assessment is norm-referenced. It allows states to peg their performance against the distribution of states. Disparagement of norms has become virtually ritual, but those who disparage them should either change their tune or explain to Finn why all of the information he wants is not useful. Second, normative information cannot be provided with tests that are used for serious accountability. Accountability will undermine the meaningfulness of norms, producing more Lake Wobegon effects.

Resnick said that educators in other countries do not apply one uniform standard for all students and are startled by the New Standards Project's proposal to do so. I say, for good reason. My politics are liberal. For generations, my family has had a commitment to working for greater equity. It is unarguable that what the American society does to certain groups of low-achieving students is unforgivable and that this needs to be changed. That the current education reform movement is finally focusing attention on what is done to those kids is a wonderful step forward.

But, at the same time, I think that if those kids are going to be helped, expectations need to be realistic. I had the privilege of living on a kibbutz many years ago, a very left-wing kibbutz. At that point, members of that kibbutz were still raising their children collectively. Little private property and no substantial disparities in wealth were allowed. The only substantial disparities in expenditures for the well-being of children were compensatory. For example, if kids had handicaps, more money was spent to buy the additional services they needed. Many of the factors that cause an unreasonable rate of school failure among certain groups in the United States—poverty, violence, hunger, doubts about the value of education, despair about the future, and so on—were absent. But there were still more able kids and fewer able kids; there were, and there always will be.

That is not to say that something unforgivable has not been done to whole groups of this population and that they have been forced to achieve less than they might and should. But some kids are more adept learners than others. Even if the political will existed to undo social inequities, some kids will learn mathematics a lot faster than others.

Although higher expectations should be set for all, focusing on one uniform set of standards is doing a disservice to children by diverting attention from one of the single most difficult problems, which is finding reasonable methods of differentiating instruction for different kinds of kids without condemning relatively low-achieving students to boring and unproductive schooling. In Great Britain, when reasonably uniform standards were imposed in the General Certificate of Secondary Education exam program before Prime Minister Margaret Thatcher's time, researchers investigating the program and teachers commenting on it said that one of the biggest problems was finding reasonable ways to differentiate instruction for students at different levels of proficiency. That is one of the key problems the U.S. reform movement faces, and it should be confronted instead of finessed with comforting slogans.

Resnick also made reference to a study that was done by the New Standards Project on the scoring of writing pieces, citing it as evidence of the ability to establish common standards among people using different assessments. I disagree with that characterization of that study. The problem the study addresses—the comparability of different assessments—is one of the most difficult ones facing the current wave of reforms. Most of the current reform movement has some degree of commitment to state, if not local, autonomy in education. Yet as Finn and others have pointed out, people nonetheless want to know—and, in some states, such as Kentucky, they are required by law to find out—how kids in their jurisdictions stack up against everyone else. The problem then becomes figuring out how to make different assessments comparable. Finn attributed doubts about the ability to equate different tests to me and my colleagues. I had nothing to do with it, and the most succinct statement of the problem antedated my time in this field. I believe it was in the early 1970s that Fred Lord said something along the lines of this: "If you think you need to equate two tests, you probably cannot."

Some steps can be taken in the direction of comparability. The question is how big those steps can be and what interpretations they will permit. The study Resnick cited attempted to address that question in one area, writing. In the study, raters from different states evaluated student writing from their own and other states, in all cases using their own scoring systems. The study showed that the ratings of any state's products by raters from that and another state were typically highly correlated, even though the raters from the second state used a different scoring system.

My argument is with Resnick's interpretation of the results. My interpretation of the results—which, I believe, is the same as that of the authors of the report—is that, in writing, people are able to agree on the relative performance of kids, which is the kind of interpretation of performance that underlies norms. Even though ratings from different states were highly correlated in the study, the average scores assigned by raters from different states were sometimes substantially different. This was particularly the case in the youngest grade in the study. Raters from some states, such as Vermont, gave higher average scores than did raters from some other states. What that means in simple English is that the raters did not agree on standards of performance. It might be possible to make them agree on standards over time, but they did not agree at that time. Moreover, this study looked only at writing. In areas such as mathematics and science, reaching comparable standards will be even more difficult, because the starting point reflects a less clear-cut agreement on what constitutes good work.

Let me address one additional specific point: teaching to the proposed new performance assessments. Resnick made a comment about giving examples from one test as preparation for another, which she said is very common in Europe. She then went on to discuss how the New Standards Project will approach that problem and said there is nothing wrong with preparing for a performance assessment by practicing the same task. In most cases, there is something very wrong with doing that. It would undermine most of the inferences about student performance that people want to make, because it would undermine the relationship of performance on that particular task to performance in the broader domain it is supposed to represent. This is one of the fundamental contradictions that need to be confronted in making the reform movement work.

Virtually everyone is agreed that, to be effective, the standards implicit in assessments have to be transparent to students, teachers, and parents. Students have to know what is expected of them. They need concrete examples of those expectations. So do teachers. That is unarguable. And the only way that can be done is by showing them student work. Work from previous exams is hardly the only source of such examples but may do well in this respect.

The problem is that, in many cases, subsequent editions of a test look alike. So, if past exams are used to illustrate to students and teachers what is expected of them, they can gradually narrow down their focus to the subset of the domain that is covered on the test and start ignoring other things.

For years, the New York State Regents Exam has been a favorite example of this issue for people on both sides of the argument about test-based accountability. On the one hand, many people credit the Regents exams with effectively raising standards, and no doubt some truth to that exists. But endless examples are available of counterproductive teaching to the Regents exams. One researcher found a geometry teacher in New York who felt that his kids could get good grades on the Regents exam by studying a very small number of types of proof, perhaps roughly a dozen, and focused a large part of his teaching on only those proofs. I remember being hauled up in front of a class and chastised because I had a trigonometry review book that was not specifically geared to the Regents exam. I was used as an example to other students of what should not be done, and the class was told that anyone who made this mistake again would face the consequences.

This is one negative side of teaching to the test. To recapitulate, what the public is interested in and what educators ought to be interested in is whether kids show a reasonable degree of mastery over big areas of performance—big domains, as the trade calls them. An important domain might be something as narrow as algebra, or it might be as broad as high school mathematics, but it will rarely be as narrow as a few tasks.

This does not mean that tests should not be used for accountability. It does mean, however, that doing so in a way that will raise standards and not simply create a different version of Lake Wobegon is an unavoidable and truly difficult challenge. Ways must be found of making these tasks concrete and transparent to students and teachers without, in essence, telling them too specifically what is on the test. This must be done in a way that makes performance on the assessment meaningful as an indicator of mastery of an important domain, not just mastery of that particular assessment. As a counterexample, if an elementary science test involves five hands-on tasks that do not change, scores will go up. People can learn to master five tasks. But what does it mean when they do? Kids could spend all year learning how to do five tasks and they would do well on that test, but they would probably know very little about science.

Resnick made a comment about avoiding teaching to the test when it creates undesirable instruction, and I think she has put her finger on one of the most critical points of what went wrong in the 1980s. When people were held accountable for performance on multiple-choice tests, the teaching to the test that resulted created not only illusory gains but also bad instruction. It involved excessive amounts of boring drill. It involved, in one local district, starting kids on test preparation materials for a third-grade test while they were still in kindergarten. It produced bad instruction, and in a very real sense, it created low, not high, standards.

But that is only one of the reasons to be worried about inappropriate teaching to the task. The other is that kids do not learn much if they are focused too narrowly on a small set of tasks. When they are, the impression of progress and of accountability are both illusory. The system lets people off the hook, and it makes people feel good without actually improving what kids know.

That is one of the central dilemmas of the current reform movement. It needs to be confronted. Saying, as many reformers do, that the problem has been solved because performance assessments are going to be used is simply wrong. Solving the problem will take far more than that.

CONCLUSION

The success of the reform movement—and specifically the use of assessments to raise standards—is going to depend on whether the political will exists to tone down expectations; to start using the evidence in-hand about the strengths and limitations of assessment; and to gather information where it is lacking. As part of the efforts to learn more, the overconfidence that characterized the 1980s must be abandoned and what happens to schools and to children when these reforms are imposed must be seriously monitored.

If educators are not realistic about this and do not look with open eyes at the evidence, the chances of success are low, and children will be the losers.

General Discussion

Diane Ravitch, as chairman and interlocutor of the panel, invited members of the panel to respond to Daniel M. Koretz's comments.

Lauren B. Resnick agreed completely that the accountability instruments and the monitoring instruments, the ones by which educators figure out if the whole reform effort is getting anywhere, must be separate. Something with a longer perspective is needed, something that can look down on the whole venture and see whether change is happening, even when people are not trying in a narrowly targeted way. That is the National Assessment of Educational Progress. Big arguments can be had about its details, but if it did not exist, educators would have to be inventing it right now.

The current system does not have standards in it. Everybody has agreed with that statement. The introduction of standards is desirable, and a very powerful way to do it is to improve the amount of accountability for what is taught and learned in class. The first line of accountability for that is student grades, teacher-given grades. That is the main place where students experience what is worth working on. That can be greatly improved to be more reliable and valid. An elegant stand-alone test can be devised. Educators must not be deterred from the improvement of accountability and grading because that is what students work for, that is what produces effort. A completely unaccountable, unfair grading system with no equating in it exists now.

Other huge steps will also have to be made. It will take the same thirty years or so, at least, to build the elegant performance system that it took to build the elegant traditional testing system, the current American testing system. It started in heavy use in the 1920s and gradually became elegant. It is a spectacular technology for what it tries to do. It is not grading; it is not accountability, not the accountability that is wanted now. Something different must be done. It can be, partly by borrowing from all that technology, but without expecting to wait thirty to forty years before it could be used.

The idea of setting a clear and absolute standard does not imply that all kids are the same. Kids will take very different amounts of time and routes to meeting the same absolute standard, and they must be given whatever they need for that, as long as they work.

It is educators' responsibility to give them that and to expect them to work and to expect enormous variability. Differences also will show up in the absolute quality of performance. An honors standard is necessary, as well as a recognition of it in this system, or else effort by some will be suppressed to bring others up. That can be done. It is not so hard.

Chester E. Finn, Jr., said that Albert Shanker's data certainly suggest that, in other countries where the distribution of basic abilities is very similar to that in the United States, a vastly larger fraction of the population can be brought to meet a much higher standard than is met here. Solving the "last child problem" is another problem worth talking about. By going from 7 percent to 50 percent, a substantial change would take place in the nature of America's performance. It would be worth doing even if it does not solve the last child problem. Another mechanism or way of thinking is needed.

Albert Shanker agreed that subjecting a youngster to a high-stakes test if the youngster has not had an opportunity to learn the material is a great injustice and worse than that. But Shanker expressed a great deal of faith that if, in the future, youngsters were headed toward a high-stakes test, the likelihood of them getting the material that would be needed to pass would be much greater than it is now.

Donald M. Stewart found the discussion rich and most timely, given what the College Board and the Educational Testing Service are going through in thinking about the future of the assessment programs in the swirling new world of national standards and assessments.

Certain values need to be protected. The old Scholastic Aptitude Test (SAT)—the reasoning part—remains an important instrument of equity. In the short run, a test like this, which is not totally congruent with curriculum, is needed. In the long run, it could be abandoned, if there were a level playing field, that all kids were being given the kind of instruction and rigorous curriculum that would enable them to have a shot at high achievement. That is not America today, but efforts should be made to move in that direction.

Other values also come into view. For example, Koretz spoke of the need for transparency of standards. The College Board and the

Educational Testing Service are about to publish proficiency tables and scales with the test scores. It will not be what students ought to know and be able to do, but what students do know and are able to do on tests, based on the reference group for the tests. The tables and scales will indicate, for example, what a 720 in math or a 640 in verbal can translate into or should translate into, based on the experiences test-takers have had.

Stewart said he was much happier when there was a bit of mystery. The pressure on kids and teacher, when the data get rolled out, is going to be tremendous. Negotiating a rigorous curriculum and taking more math and higher-level courses in the social sciences and humanities results in higher scores. Contrary to what Resnick feels about the SAT, a relationship exists between effort and rigor and the student's score. Students who take rigorous courses get better scores. But to make this more congruent with curriculum so that it can be more of an accountability measure is very bothersome. One of the great strengths of the SAT is that it cannot be used to hold teachers accountable for what they teach.

Perhaps an old-fashioned desire to maintain some degree of academic freedom is at play. Teachers ought to be free to interpret, experiment, and be creative and not have the hammer of a test that their students are to learn over their heads. That was not the kind of teaching and the kind of experience earlier generations had.

Educators should not be worried as much about accountability as they should about enhancing teaching and learning, and this particular test was not designed for that. In the whole national debate, great confusion exists over what formative assessment is and what summative assessment is. An effort has been made to translate the kind of assessment that may help in the teaching and the learning process. Or the effort may confound matters. The jury is still out.

Trying to take those measures and those approaches when designing summative tests is adding to the confusion. Certain tests are going to be either passed or failed. But arbitrary cutoff scores are not good; there should always be a range. There is going to be some selection, and those are somewhat different tests.

Finn then asked, without disputing the reasoning behind needing two different kinds of tests—one for accountability purposes and one for monitoring purposes—how is an educator ever going to explain to a parent or to a legislator why both kinds have to be taken by kids and paid for by the taxpayer? How will this be made transparent to normal people?

In answering, Koretz explained what he has told people in the political world. Over time, most tests that are used for accountability are going to become degraded in one way or another. Educators are unlikely to be able to stay in front of all the undesired effects of teaching to those tests. Periodically, they will need to be recalibrated, redesigned, and so on. That is one of the functions of an audit test.

Resnick commented that the word *audit* is what people understand.

A person would not want a computer from some distance to compute his taxes. However, nobody believes that, without tax auditing, everybody would, over time, stay honest. So, something is needed that is close to the people doing the paying, who have a chance to say, "Here is what I earned and here is what I think I owe." And, something is needed that is a little further away that keeps people doing that in a way that the public can believe.

Finn added the caveat that no individual member of the public wants to be the subject of the audit.

Resnick said that is true, but people accept that it needs to be done.

Lawrence Gladieux, of the College Board, suggested that a number of European countries seem to be moving in the direction of curriculum-free testing. At least, that is the drift of some of the thinking. This may not be to the point where ministries are formally moving in that direction, but international discussions seem to be pointing that way. They are, at least, looking at the SAT and saying: "Gee, I wish we could create something like that here, but we don't have the tradition."

Gladieux wondered if some of the invoking of the comparative experience in other countries idealizes what is going on abroad. The report by Lynne Cheney from the National Endowment for the Humanities about testing in different countries was misleading in terms of the cultural context and the population of students who took the tests.

Koretz added that a lot of European countries have reached the point where they avoid high-stakes exams below the teenage years. Switzerland still has a grade five exam, but most of them no longer do it. Proposals are not being floated in the United States to emulate them anyway.

Exams with stakes in countries such as Germany and France have had a substantial effect on instruction. Whether those effects are net positive or negative and the extent to which they have influenced international comparisons is arguable. Debates have been held in the countries that have used these exams for a long time—for many decades—about what the mix of positive and negative effects is.

To pick one difference between countries, such as exams, and say that that must explain the difference in achievement is also methodologically foolish. A group of Japanese professionals who live in Koretz's neighborhood and whose kids go to the schools that his kids go to like the local schools more than he does. They also expressed an antipathy for the Japanese examination system. Some of them maintained that one of the reasons that many Japanese parents buy their way into private schools is to avoid the exams. So, what the effect overall has been is questionable.

By the way, in the Japanese example, it is worth asking the question: "Why is it that Japanese-American kids, for example, and Chinese-American kids in the United States, absent the stakes that Shanker says are needed and absent the examination system that is present in Japan, still outscore Anglos." The answer is fairly obvious.

Shanker suggested they have not been Americanized yet.

Koretz countered that many of them have, according to other indications, but some of the cultural differences persist.

Koretz then asserted that Shanker had given a very Skinnerian line about the role of extrinsic rewards, with which he partly agreed, but then raised two caveats.

People now say that lifelong learning should be a concern; that is, what learning people do after that of school. If a system is built in which the motivation toward work in school is the tests they get at the end of it, educators have not done a very good job.

The Skinnerian would say that the job of behavior modification is to wean people from dependence on extrinsic rewards. A whole host of research in social psychology—a very confusing body of research—suggests that, under certain circumstances, excessive reliance on extrinsic rewards undermines, instead of reinforces, intrinsic motivation. James Fallows reports that if you wait for a subway at rush hour in Singapore, you will see all the salary men standing around posters of difficult math problems that the government has put up there for their entertainment. They are not being tested. While some consequences are necessary, a wholesale reliance on extrinsic reward is likely to be counterproductive.

Shanker retorted that he is not very Skinnerian. If he were provided with a very high incentive to pick up garbage along a certain street, he might, if he needed the money, pick it up. As soon as the payments stopped, he would stop picking up the garbage. However, he might open a book by Shakespeare for the first time because of an extrinsic reward, complaining all the while. But after reading one or two plays, he might watch some plays on television and go to some and begin enjoying them. Whether one moves to some intrinsic enjoyment of the activity is crucial. Some are going to continue to be extrinsic; they are just not pleasurable or exciting or appealing to the intellect.

Shanker favors using all incentives, a range of incentives. With respect to every policy except education in America—welfare mothers, out-of-wedlock pregnancies, or all sorts of other problems—incentives are talked about. In everything but education, society believes that if you change the incentives, you will change the behavior and outcomes.

A small percentage—3, 4, 5, 6, or 7 percent—of kids are apt to perform in the highest level of whatever test. European tests are passed by 36 percent of the people who sit for one or two full days writing essays or solving problems. Why was at least 36 percent of another nation's student population, as against 3 percent or 7 percent of the U.S. student population, able to reach high performance?

The American Federation of Teachers (AFT) intends to follow up with a close look at some of the assessments and stakes used in other countries for the group that is not going to college, to show that they are not just taking their top 40 or 45 percent and throwing the rest away but that they are doing something with all their youngsters. No other country in the world, whether developed or undeveloped, does not have clear stakes attached to educational outcomes. What is the United States doing? American kids are being destroyed. Stakes send clear messages. What are the outcomes? What is in it for me? What will happen if I do not do it? What will happen if I do do it?

When Shanker started with the United Federation of Teachers, it was a very small organization in New York City that had been around for a long time and had 2,000 members. It has grown to more than 100,000. He does not assume that people only wanted salary increases. He spends time with people and discusses thirty or forty different types of motivation, to find out their interests and problems. Nothing can be built unless the entire range of things that move people is dealt with. This is not done in education. Tests and high stakes are not the only thing that are neglected in schools in terms of reaching children.

Stephen P. Heyneman of the World Bank said that he has done a number of international studies. He would not invest in a country that did not have high-stakes exams. It would not be a worthwhile investment. Therefore, he would not recommend exportation of the SAT. However, he knows of no country that wants to import it, except for its psychometric properties. That is a different story. Meanwhile, examinations and the technology of examinations are a very big export product of the United States.

Heyneman agreed with the comparisons of how other countries do exams. A danger exists of oversimplifying how other countries organize their exams. In some cases, while they have very high-stakes exams, they are also, independently—Britain is a good example—trying to have national tests separate from those exams. A controversy is brewing in Britain now, with teachers refusing to give them. So, it is not all unidimensional. Their high performance is not all because they have good high-stakes exams.

The comparison of European exams with the Advanced Placement (AP) exam is a little risky because a number of other high-quality academic exams are used in the United States and to suggest that the AP is the only high-quality academic exam is overdrawn. Using the AP exam as representative of the full gamut of high-stakes exams in the United States is problematic.

The Russians would be fascinated by this conversation. They have quickly become a federal system in the field of education. They now have all local control and all local financing right down to the personal income tax financing of all compulsory and vocational education. They need to come up to speed on how to organize themselves in their local areas. They would be very confused, though, by this dialogue. Much of the terminology is confusing. A number of terms have been invented and are used particularly in an American audience. A domestic, almost parochial, fascination can be found with the idiosyncracies of these various issues.

In a federal system, control of the educational process cannot be unidimensional. However, stakes in the system are necessary. Like it or not, educators are operating in a federal system, and education is very much a local matter. In spite of the enormity of the Goals 2000 legislation, in percentage terms and in terms of the American budget and where the money is coming from, the schools are a local business and local people are going to look askance if the standards are being set by people who are being paid by other sources with money other than local tax dollars. That is reality. Common sense ought to prevail, and there ought to be some compromise. High stakes are needed, as well as a feedback mechanism and voluntarism in the system.

Thomas E. Mann, of the Brookings Institution, contended that Shanker's argument about stakes is utterly convincing, perhaps the most compelling argument made at the conference. He asked for guidance as to how to move the educational system from where it is today to where educators would like it to be with respect to stakes for college and stakes for jobs.

Ravitch offered one answer. In New York City, the chancellor created a commission made up, mainly, of major employers—the chairman of the New York Stock Exchange, the chairman of Brooklyn Union Gas, the head of the telephone company, the chancellor of City University, the president of other institutions of higher education—as well as union leaders, parent spokesmen, and representatives from different parts of the community. Everyone is concerned about standards because everybody knows the dire numbers on the New York City school system. A positive move would be an agreement that the employers will do what Shanker suggested, which is to ask for a transcript. That is, the school system has to devise a transcript that employers will look at and understand. It would not be the same transcript, necessarily, that is sent to colleges.

The objective is to get the employers on board, recognizing that they have a social responsibility. City University has been moving rapidly toward developing the College Preparatory Initiative, which lets students know in advance: "If you want to go to a senior college, this is what you have to be able to do. These are the courses you have to take." City University has produced the research showing that scores on entry exams are directly related to the number of academic courses taken in high school. The more academic courses a student takes, the better she will do on the exams. With each additional course taken in high school, the higher the pass rate of the students. Both universities and employers need to agree that they must set standards for students so that they understand that doing well in school is important for college and work.

Robert B. Schwartz, from the Pew Charitable Trusts, pointed out the schizophrenia in the discussion. Education is, principally, a local responsibility and yet, as Eugenia Kemble cited, the clear pressure even from within the ranks of teachers is for a more national system and more national standards. Polling data support that. That is not inconsistent even with what Deborah Wadsworth reported.

Because of America's traditions and because more than 90 percent of the funding and the statutory framework for education is state and local, limits are imposed on how much of a federal role will exist.

When Sizer and Stewart warn about unwarranted federal intrusion, on the one side, and Finn says, in effect, that Goals 2000 is a kind of a copout and that educators have abandoned any serious attempt to create enough of a common data system to make comparisons, on the other, what that says is that probably for now Goals 2000 is the best that can be gotten. It also underscores an important point that Finn made, which is that the action, principally, is in the states. One reason that the New Standards Project, for example, is so important in the system is that what it says is that the states—again, for the reasons that Finn cited—want meaningful comparisons. The states are not going to wait around for a political consensus to be formed that expresses itself in national legislation. The states are saying: "We are going to work together to figure out some way that balances our own desires for differentiation, that preserves our right to develop our own reform strategies, but which, at the end of the line, does enable us to make comparisons."

Oregon's approach to school reform is one of the most radical in the country. The reforms are based upon the notion that the principal responsibility of the system is to prepare all kids for a lifetime of further learning and work. Oregon has developed a two-tiered certificate system and has, effectively, abolished tracking and moved away from saying, "Some kids are going to be prepared for college, and some are going to be prepared for work." The reforms are being driven, in a substantial measure, by business leadership, governmental leadership, and educational leadership in the state.

The college system in Oregon, suddenly confronted with the reality of not having transcripts of the sort historically depended upon, has begun to figure out that the entrance system must be realigned or redesigned and that proficiencies must be defined for entrants that will, in effect, match the new certification standard that is going to be required for graduation. Employers are beginning to struggle with the same kind of question. They will require a political coming together—higher education, business, education, and government—to begin to deal realistically with what Shanker, in particular, has been calling for.

Shanker said that, if college entry is key, the federal government is the major player in terms of loans and grants. The federal government is now and will become a major player in school-to-work transition.

Part of the problem is that the United States wanted to expand opportunities after World War II for further education, and it was done in a sloppy way. Thought was not given to the different purposes of different institutions and the incentives for entry. The result, unfortunately, is that many four-year institutions must shop and compete for students, basically telling them: "Come on in, we need you; you don't have to work very hard; we have good swimming pools."

A good part of higher education is not holding up standards and is not, primarily, academic. Colleges and universities are in business, and they are in business to fill seats. They are not very well equipped to do remedial work, which they are doing more and more.

If something were to be put together nationally that would clearly indicate that moves are being made toward equity and that opportunity is opening up for further and lifelong education, a system that made more sense in providing more opportunities and more sensible opportunities, then everyone would have second chances.

The high schools in European systems were considered elitist twenty years ago. They were systems that had only 15 percent of the youngsters meeting standards. How did they go from 15 percent to 40 or 15 percent to 36 without changing the standards very much? People are not going over there to say, "Hey, look, Australians and French, we were right when we called you elitist; look at what you have done; you have now surpassed us; you are now the system that produces."

The United States has lots of people in colleges because standards were abandoned. It was done the easy way. The question of college and further education must be dealt with. Federal loans, grants, and institutional aid must be used as a federal policy toward creating incentives and do it in a way that expands opportunities and second chances so that no one can say the purpose of this is to move toward an elitist system and to push people who really need an education out of the system. The elementary and secondary schools alone cannot reform themselves. The problem lies in the employment sector and in the higher education sector. Those are the control points.

At one time, more than 200,000 school boards were functioning in America; there are 15,000 now, largely as a result of consolidation. Why did every high school in the country have Carnegie units—a period of English and so on? Because those subjects were what the colleges decided they needed for entry standards. Even though a high degree of decentralization exists in the United States, Carnegie units became the pattern for high school education. That is how powerful college entry standards are.

Some policy is needed, and the federal government has a big role to play in formulating it. A carefully developed system is needed that is connected with the work system. Colleges cannot be expected to do it, because if one college raises standards, the customers move to another one that does not have standards.

Conflicts abound on the subject of excellence versus equity. Arguments are made that they are consistent with each other, but no policies demonstrate a faith that they are. For example, industries, unions, and civil rights interests are going to develop standards for various jobs. "What do you need to be a good welder or to be a good tool and die maker?" In Goals 2000 is a statement that an employer, accused of discrimination, may not use, as a defense, the hiring of an employee on the basis that the employee met the federal employment standards for that particular category. On the one hand, there is an incentive: "We create a standard. We are defining it. We are getting all the partners in there." On the other hand, the message is: "But if you hire a person who meets the standard, you cannot use it as a defense in court unless you also meet your affirmative action objectives." The result is a state of conflict.

Ravitch pointed out that the National Center for Education Statistics projects that, by the year 2004, high school enrollment will increase between 20 and 25 percent, which may provide the opportunity to set standards. The colleges will not be fighting over every warm body because so many of them will be available.

Stewart added that demographics would have had some influence, and with the uptick in the eighteen-to-twenty-one-year-old cohort, some colleges will be able to develop more selective admissions standards.

The federal government is part of the problem and created some of the problem through the 1972 amendments to the higher education act, which targeted aid on students. It was designed to have institutions at the mercy of the marketplace. A major struggle ensued in the early years.

Representative Edith Green was the champion of the One Dupont Circle organizations, which wanted the aid to go directly to institutions, not students. The established interest lost, and since then federal aid goes directly to the students instead of the colleges and universities. Many institutions—particularly those that are almost totally dependent on federal aid—cannot say no. They cannot afford it.

They have no other sources of income. The time has come in this new framework, with these thoughts with regard to both equity and excellence, to reconsider the mix between institutional and student-targeted aid because institutions are at the mercy of the marketplace.

Ravitch commented that in K-12 the framework for financial assistance is the opposite; all the aid is institutional, and none of it goes directly to students.

Stewart replied that that does not work, either.

Conference Participants
with their affiliations at the time of the conference

Henry J. Aaron*
Brookings Institution

Jeanne Allen
Center for Education Reform

Janice K. Anderson
U.S. Department of Education

Andrea Baird

Janet Baldwin
GED Testing

John Barth
Committee on Education and Labor,
*   U.S. House of Representatives*

Paul Barton
Educational Testing Service

Beatrice F. Birman
U.S. General Accounting Office

David Boaz
Cato Institute

Larry S. Bowen
George Mason University

Margaret Branson
Center for Civic Education

David W. Breneman*
Harvard University

Dianne C. Brown
American Psychological Association

Robert W. Brown
National Aeronautics and Space
*   Administration*

John H. Burkett
U.S. Department of Education

Gene R. Carter
Association of Supervision and
*   Curriculum Development*

Jennifer Cetta
Education Daily

David Chester
Education Reports

Joseph Conaty
U.S. Department of Education

Christopher T. Cross
Business Roundtable

Glen W. Cutlip
National Education Association

William F. Davis, OSFS
U.S. Catholic Conference

Karen Diegmueller
Education Week

Denis P. Doyle
Hudson Institute

Russell Edgerton
American Association for Higher
*   Education*

Emerson J. Elliott
National Center for Education Statistics

Penelope Engel
Educational Testing Service

Julie I. Englund*
Brookings Institution

Lawrence W. Feinberg
National Assessment Governing Board

Michael J. Feuer
National Academy of Sciences

Donna Fowler
American Federation of Teachers

Kathleen Fulton
*Office of Technology Assessment,
United States Congress*

Matthew Gandal
American Federation of Teachers

James D. Gates
*National Council of Teachers of
Mathematics*

Alan Ginsburg
U.S. Department of Education

Lawrence E. Gladieux
College Board

Susan Mandel Glazer
International Reading Association

Claudia Goldin*
Brookings Institution

Karen Goldman
American Federation of Teachers

Dorothy Goodman
*International Schools Journal, World
History Association, COMPASS*

Daniel Gursky
American Federation of Teachers

Drue Shropshire Guy
*Quality Education for Minorities
(QEM) Network*

Merrie Hahn
*National Association of Elementary
Schools Principals*

Samuel Halperin
American Youth Policy Forum

Jane Hannaway
The Urban Institute

Arthur M. Hauptman

Angela Henkels
Center for Education Reform

James Herbert
*National Endowment for the
Humanities*

Stephen P. Heyneman
The World Bank

Charles Hokanson
American Federation of Teachers

David G. Imig
*American Association of Colleges for
Teacher Education*

Carol Innerst
Washington Times

Jack Jennings
*Committee on Education and Labor,
United States House of
Representatives*

Sylvia T. Johnson
Howard University

Mary Jordan
Washington Post

Eugenia Kemble
American Federation of Teachers

Breene M. Kerr*
Brookside Company

Jacqueline King
College Board

Victor Klatt
*Committee on Education and Labor,
U.S. House of Representatives*

Charles Kolb

David D. Kumar
Florida Atlantic University

Martharose F. Laffey
National Council for the Social Studies

Annette Licitra
Education Daily

Richard Long
International Reading Association

James Mahoney
American Association of Community Colleges

Shirley Malcom
American Association for the Advancement of Science

Thomas E. Mann*
Brookings Institution

Joyce G. McCray
Council for American Private Education

Catherine McNamee
National Catholic Educational Association

Michael F. McPherson*
Williams College

Ann Meyer
The McKenzie Group

Patricia B. Mitchell
Center for Excellence in Education

Mark J. Molli
Center for Civic Education

Ken Nelson
National Education Goals Panel

Martin E. Orland
National Education Goals Panel

Gary W. Phillips
U.S. Department of Education

Lanny Proffer
National Geographic Society

Charles Quigley
Center for Civic Education

Marcia Reecer
American Federation of Teachers

Mindy C. Reiser

Peter D. Relic
National Association of Independent Schools

Lois Dickson Rice*
Brookings Institution

Bella Rosenberg
American Federation of Teachers

Iris Rotberg
National Science Foundation

Amy Schwartz
Washington Post

Robert B. Schwartz
Pew Charitable Trusts

Ramsay Selden
Council of Chief State School Officers

Duane Smith
Center for Civic Education

Joyce Smith
National Association of College Admissions Counselors

Peter Smith
George Washington University

Gerald Sroufe
American Educational Research Association

Dena G. Stoner
CEDaR

Susan Traiman
National Governors' Association

Roy Truby
*National Assessment of Educational
    Progress Governing Board*

Deborah Wadsworth
Public Agenda Foundation

Ruth Wattenberg
American Federation of Teachers

Basil Whiting
Public/Private Ventures

Alexandra K. Wigdor
*National Research Council, National
    Academy of Sciences*

Stephanie Willerton
U.S. Department of Education

Claudia Winkler
Scripps-Howard News Service

John Wirt
Office of Technology Assessment

Emily Wurtz
National Education Goals Panel

*Advisory Committee member,
    Brookings Institution Brown Center
    on Education Policy*